Dear Beloved Readers,

I met Jeanette Morgan about 15 years ago through a mutual friend and little did we know how beautifully our relationship would blossom. About 7 years ago our friendship took a turn when we began walking the neighborhood for some good old fashioned exercise. God used this opportunity for me to share the love of Jesus with her and we've never been the same. Those early walks were only the very beginning of what would become a truly authentic friendship as we discovered walking in grace together. I've watched her grow in wisdom, discernment and understanding–but equally if not more important; love, compassion and humility. Jeanette operates in a seer gift and God speaks to her through many dreams and visions. What she writes is truly revelatory and will allow you to be refreshed at the way God's creativity of explaining his truth dances off the pages. She listens for the voice of our King and helps guide others to that deeper place of intimacy.

—Trena M. Ratto
Founder & CEO
Passion for Purpose Ministries
Livermore, CA

Jeanette Morgan is what one would call a "modern day psalmist". Her writings are so inspired by the Holy Spirit that they are truly life changing. Not only will her written words minister to you in spirit, soul, and body, but they will also confirm prophetic words spoken over your life through other prophets of God. This book is definitely a must read. You will truly be uplifted and blessed.

—Patricia L. Garner, Senior Pastor
In His Image Int'l Ministries
Antioch, California

God called Jeanette and I praise him that she answered. Jeanette is a woman after God's heart. She walks in the fruits of the spirit and through the hard times she will stand on the word and not let go. She is a women blessed by God to be used to translate for God through writings and to be a blessing to so many people. Jeanette has taken a decrease and God has caused such a spiritual increase in her life. She is a woman of integrity, dependability and great trust. His anointed power is upon her and these inspirational writings. It is an honor and pleasure to have crossed paths with Jeanette in this life for such a time as this. To God be all the glory! Jeanette you are a star exploding on earth for Jesus!

"To whom much is given much is required." (Luke 12:48)

—Antoinette Smith, Associate Pastor
Genesis Upperroom Church International
Saratoga, California.

While studying these writings during our devotions, my mother and I gained further insight into what is taking place in the supernatural and what God seems to be doing despite the on-goings in the world. We always finished feeling stronger spiritually. It was as if God had Jeanette write those inspirations tailored specifically for what we needed to uplift our spirits. As believers we know inevitably that if we want to be all we can be in Christ and for Christ we will have to endure some desert seasons. Jeanette's writings inspired by the Holy Spirit helped us to know that God is still in control no matter what we are in the midst of.

—Minjoy Cato
San Jose, California

THE
VOICE
THAT MUST BE
HEARD

THE
VOICE
THAT MUST BE
HEARD

Awakening your
Heart, Mind, and
Spirit Through the
Power of Divine
Revelation

JEANETTE C MORGAN

TATE PUBLISHING & *Enterprises*

Published by Tate Publishing & Enterprises, LLC
127 E. Trade Center Terrace | Mustang, Oklahoma 73064 USA
1.888.361.9473 | www.tatepublishing.com

Tate Publishing is committed to excellence in the publishing industry. The company reflects the philosophy established by the founders, based on Psalm 68:11,
"The Lord gave the word and great was the company of those who published it."

Book design copyright © 2009 by Tate Publishing, LLC. All rights reserved.
Cover design by Kandi Evans
Interior design by Nathan Harmony

Published in the United States of America

ISBN: 978-1-60696-649-5
Religion: Biblical Studies: Bible Study Guides
09.12.03

Foreword

In each of our lives God has chosen us and has given us a directive to present His word in truth. The talents, the abilities, along with the gifts of the Holy Spirit that He alone imparts into our lives are provided so we can present to those who have an ear to hear, words of inspiration to edify, encourage, strengthen, to bring comfort, to build us up in our most Holy faith. Along with this directive comes a great responsibility for each one of us to step out in the faith of God and freely give back to His people for the sole purpose of continual intimacy with the heart of the Father. The inspirational insight of revelation and knowledge given to Jeanette Morgan will nourish your spirit, strengthen your soul and reach deep into your heart with a desire to seek the heart of God to understand His love, His grace, His mercy and compassion for humanity. To inspire the body of Christ and to all of those who are seeking the truth in developing a relationship with a living God.

—Michael Galletta
Senior Pastor
Genesis Upperroom Church International
Saratoga , CA

Dedication

This book is dedicated to my Lord and Savior Jesus Christ, for without him and all he encompasses, I would not be walking in the new life and divinely created destiny he died to give me, nor would I have this book to share with others to encourage them in the same way.

Acknowledgments

I would like to thank the ministers at Genesis Upperroom Church International in Saratoga, California. Without their life-giving manna from the Holy Spirit, I would not have pressed through and stayed the course. There are no words to express my appreciation and gratitude for the bottomless well of living water I have received there throughout my spiritual walk.

As well I am in great appreciation to all of the many men and women of God whose ministry conferences I have attended. I have received such a wealth of knowledge and understanding, and I feel so privileged to have sat under their teachings and received the anointing God has dispensed through those individuals, also for giving of themselves so they can pave the way for the rest of us up and coming in the body of Christ.

I would be remiss if I did not mention my friends in the faith—dear sisters and brothers, who loved me, guided me, prayed for me, and encouraged me by displaying God's love, grace, and mercy. You *know* who each of you are. I greatly value the gifts and qualities the Lord has fashioned in you and respect you as mighty teachers, prophets, and prophetesses of God. I could not get through the challenges and spiritual battles thus far without your support in the many ways you have provided.

A big thank you to my husband and my children for loving me and adding so much value to my life, for without you I would not be as rich in love as I am.

Thank you to all my family members for your love and for providing precious memories in my life through the years.

To my publisher and all those involved that worked so hard to bring this book to its destiny, I thank you for recognizing the move of God through me in these writings and your commitment in assisting me to maintain this work as "God's book." All for his glory!

May God bless all of those abundantly for loving me and praying for me through this life!

Contents

Introduction

Throughout the entire year of 2007 and the beginning of 2008, the Lord began prompting me to write down the revelations he was giving me by his Spirit. I was instructed to send them out to others in the body of Christ not knowing until later that God was calling me to assemble these writings into a book. I discovered greater depth and experienced personal revelation of our Lord and Savior through these times of writing, and today I share them with you. The purpose is that you would be built up to understand God's love for you. His desire is for you to step out of the realm of religious traditions, lingo, and man-made yokes into his holy atmosphere of revelation. This divine revelation is so important if we are to become the Bride of Christ he calls us to be. The Spirit of God beckons us to become that bride without spot or wrinkle through the power of illuminating our hearts, minds, and spirits to his truth, his way, and his life.

Revelation is like an explosion of God's wisdom, knowledge, understanding, and vision in one. So many of us have walked in a dim world of Christianity or a false representation of it not truly knowing the heart of our King for us and find ourselves stuck, frustrated, and unable to overcome. We often view the church as one without power to help us in our desperate need. But that is all about to change. One of my favorite scriptures in the Bible is "when darkness overtakes the godly, light will come bursting in" (Psalm 112:4, NLT).

My friends, the church has lived in darkness for too long, and she must be inspired once again, ignited once again, and blaze with passion through the light of revelation that Christ is dispensing in this end-time harvest. We are called to *be* the church's finest hour. It is an hour where the church arises to be all she was created for, that she would shine like a beacon in the storm for all those who are looking for the way to salvation. It's not about perfecting ourselves but living in the truth that transforms us to a new way of living—a life filled with freedom and joy, knowing that we each were created with a destiny, a divine purpose for the kingdom of heaven. My personal prayer is that when you read this collection of Holy Spirit-inspired writings, you will discover the great love and passion the Lord has for you as an individual and that this love he has for you will cause you to soar. And with each individual this revelation empowers, it will ignite another and another to draw us in unity as a great army for the kingdom. There is a voice that must be heard. It is the voice of the Spirit of God. We must listen to his voice and respond to it by positioning ourselves to follow it. When we move in faith to what we have heard, we will illuminate the church for the world to see her in all Christ's glory.

Look! I stand at the door and knock. If you hear my voice and open the door, I will come in, and we will share a meal together as friends. Those who are victorious will sit with me on my throne, just as I was victorious and sat with my Father on his throne. Anyone with ears to hear must listen to the Spirit and understand what he is saying to the churches.

Revelations 3:20–22 (NLT)

Part One

Revelation for
Your Heart

The Voice That Must Be Heard

Each of us carries a voice inside of us. I'm not referring to the sound that comes from our mouths; our voice boxes. I'm referring to the voice that lies deep in every man's spirit. These are the cries that don't form the words to express themselves. Some of these are deep cries of pain, of bondage, of creativity desiring to be birthed or expressions of an overwhelming love—secrets locked inside, undiscovered, unknown to another. This voice is so deep no one hears it except you...or so you think. But God hears that deep cry in your spirit. He knows it, he hears it, and he moves on behalf of it.

When Adam and Eve sinned, and the Lord removed them from the Garden of Eden, he already knew the cry in their spirit. He moved on behalf of that cry by prophesying the coming Messiah to redeem man back unto the Lord. God sensed the cry in their spirit because *his* spirit lived in them. They were God-breathed. He heard, not with words but in a language only he knows, the voice of the spirit in them anguishing over their mistake. They had been deceived.

How many of us have made choices in our lives that we wish we had never made? Choices made in hastiness by not seeking God first, choices out of sheer desperation, or choices that we made because we were just plain deceived. God hears it. He hears the regret in our spirit, the anguish from our poor decision. He listens for the repentant heart and the voice that cries out for his forgiveness, his grace, his mercy, his salvation.

Cain felt dejected because the Lord didn't accept his offering (Genesis 4:5). God heard the dismay in the voice of Cain's spirit man and warned him to be careful as his rejection turned to anger and jealousy. God told Cain to be careful, "for evil is knocking at your door." God knew this because he heard it in Cain's spirit.

Cain killed his brother Abel (Genesis 4:10). God knew this not because he *saw*—although we know from Scripture that God does see all—but I believe God wanted to emphasize that he *heard* the voice of Abel's blood, his life, his spirit cry out to God for justice. The life in Abel's blood was the life of God's breath, for he took the dust of the earth and breathed into man his life.

God is a God of justice. He is our vindicator, and he is our shield. He hears the voice of our spirit man, for he knows the very nature of that voice—himself. He *is* justice.

We all have a voice inside of us that longs to be free, to soar, and to sing. God put that spirit in us. But it is the enemy of our souls, Satan, who wants to bind up the voice, to stifle it, to smother it, because he knows that the true voice when released, damages the plans of his dark kingdom. This is the voice of truth. It is what is real, factual. The voice of truth sheds light, life, and hope. The voice of truth exposes the devil and reveals him as a liar, a deceiver. Truth compels us to move forward, to pursue because truth is the one who lives in us.

From the very fall of man that voice was bound up in law until Jesus came to set it free by becoming the sin, the ultimate sacrifice, and the redemption. In a body of flesh and the spirit of the Father, Jesus was the voice of God that passed judgment upon sin, declared the kingdom of darkness defeated, and set prisoners free. He was the voice of man crying out in desperation for a savior. Jesus became the voice for man and for God. He was grace.

What is the voice in your spirit man crying out for? Is it crying out for freedom, justice, love, acceptance, mercy, or healing? Every spirit longs to be free; every spirit desires to be heard.

There was a bleeding woman, one who had been shunned, shamed, and misunderstood. Others had given up hope for her. But there was a voice inside of her, a cry so desperate for deliverance, for salvation from her iniquity and her despair. It was the voice *in* her, the cry *in* her that gave her the force to push past the obstacles in her way and reach out in complete abandonment to the one who could restore her soul. The Father heard the voice of her spirit man crying out, and he moved on behalf of it. He moved on behalf of it when he sent *his* voice, Jesus, to the earth to *be* her answer.

The Father knows the voice deep in our spirit; he

knows because he put it there long ago when he breathed that part of him into us—the life. When life is withering, when it is dying, it releases a voice, a cry, a sound in the spiritual realm that is noticed. God's Word says that not one sparrow falls to the ground without him noticing. It may not be noticed by others in the natural because it is not verbal. But God notices the voice without words, and he moves from his throne and bends his ear down to hear the sound. He responds by sending his own sound, his own cry, his very voice that says *I AM!*

We, the church, are given a message to carry in us on this earth. It's *his* voice, *his* message. We are to be carriers of the voice of God. As we are in him and he is in us, it is his voice that moves in us and compels us to move on behalf of another. When we listen to the voice deep inside, he directs us to the cries that we may be the vessels through which he answers—vessels in which God takes from his supernatural realm and invades the natural exactly the way Jesus did. He became the vessel in which God took from heaven and delivered to the earth that the earth may be delivered back unto the Father. One cry, one answer, one drop of blood; life that healed the earth that we may live in his realm once again, just as Adam and Eve before the fall. There is a voice that needs to be heard, for a hurting and perishing world needs it. It is the voice of love which is *himself*.

> Against its will, all creation was subjected to God's curse. But with eager hope, the creation looks forward to the day when it will join God's children

in glorious freedom from death and decay. For we know that all creation has been groaning as in the pains of childbirth right up to the present time. And we believers also groan, even though we have the Holy Spirit within us as a foretaste of future glory, for we long for our bodies to be released from sin and suffering. We, too, wait with eager hope for the day when God will give us our full rights as his adopted children, including the new bodies he has promised us. We were given this hope when we were saved. If we already have something, then we don't need to hope for it. But if we look forward to something we don't yet have, we must wait patiently and confidently.

And the Holy Spirit helps us in our weakness. For example, we don't know what God wants us to pray for. But the Holy Spirit prays for us with groanings that cannot be expressed in words. And the Father who knows all hearts knows what the Spirit is saying, for the Spirit pleads for us believers in harmony with God's own will. And we know that God causes everything to work together for the good of those who love God and are called according to his purpose for them. For God knew his people in advance, and he chose them to become like his Son, so that his Son would be the firstborn among many brothers and sisters. And having chosen them, he called them to come to him. And having called them, he gave them right standing with himself. And having given them right standing, he gave them his glory.

Romans 8:20–30

Tough Love
is True Love

This is what the Lord, the God of Israel says: "The good figs represent the exiles I sent from Judah to the land of the Babylonians. I have sent them into captivity for their own good. I will see that they are well treated, and I will bring them back here again. I will build them up and not tear them down. I will plant them and not uproot them. I will give them hearts that will recognize me as the Lord. They will be my people and I will be their God, for they will return to me wholeheartedly."

Jeremiah 24:5–7

God will often send us into "captivity" for our own good. It doesn't always make sense at the time; however, God has the better view and the better plan and purpose—to turn hearts wholly to him.

Many of us have been or are currently held captive by our circumstances, our lack of finances, lack of opportunity, held captive by not being able to take control of something for ourselves, or change our own situations, such as job situation or an illness. It doesn't feel good when we are held back from what *we* want to do or what *we* have planned. Sometimes we are held captive by an inability to move forward with a dream or a plan or a certain lifestyle that we want to live.

You see God loves you so much and he wants the best for you that he's willing to allow you to be held captive for a time. Sometimes it's to keep from doing further harm to ourselves or to others. Most often it's to keep us from going down a path of destruction to lose our very own souls.

When we are held captive by our circumstances, it allows us the opportunity to see things differently, from a different perspective, God's view, and to recognize that we can't help ourselves. We recognize that we don't have control. We don't have the power in ourselves. It reveals our inadequacy. It prevents self-sufficiency, a path that will lead us away from God instead of to him.

Does this sound mean? Do you wonder why a God who says he is good allows us to be held captive? Let's look at Jesus as the ultimate example. To our own minds we wonder, *Why would a good God allow Jesus to be held captive, to be beaten, bruised, whipped, speared, and crucified?* He submitted his own life into the hands of his enemies—the very people he sacrificed himself to save. It didn't make sense to many on the ground watching this gruesome event take place. But God had a plan; he had a purpose beyond our own understanding (Proverbs 3:5). It was beyond even the devil's own understanding.

While watching an interview on a television morning show one day, I saw they were interviewing a young man who was a self-proclaimed Satanist. He balked at the name of Jesus when the interviewer asked him why he was so opposed to Jesus. The young man said he could never believe in a God who would murder his own son. As I sat and watched, I felt so sad. I felt so sad because like this self-proclaimed Satanist, many others had missed the point. God didn't do it to be cruel; he did it for love. He loved us way too much to see us experience eternal punishment, eternal pain, eternal abuse, eternal suffering. So he took it on himself. People forget that Jesus was more than man, a prophet; he was God in the flesh. You see that self-proclaimed Satanist was blinded and ignorant due to the enemy's deception that God's love was so overwhelming for his children, so powerful that he sent himself into this world and suffered on our behalf that we could live in fellowship, in relationship with him for all eternity (1 John 5:20).

That is *tough love*, my friends. It's tough to love like that—to love others who persecute you, who condemn you, who have abused you, worn out their welcome, who stomped on your heart, lied to you, used you, and caused you so much pain and anguish in your heart. Do you remember being hurt by someone you loved, you cared for, you trusted? The pain can be deep; it can be gut-wrenching, and devastating.

Now for just a moment while you are remembering how that felt, imagine for a moment how you think Jesus felt when we did all these things to him? And we all have, all before we came to know him and still sometimes even though we know him (Isaiah 53:6). The Bible says despite what we did to put him on that cross—and every one of us has had a hand in that—he took the punishment willingly (Luke 26:39). He sacrificed himself for those who didn't recognize that he did it to save them from punishment of their own sins.

Think about this for a moment. How would you feel if someone came in and deceived your child and told them, "No, don't worry. This stuff won't hurt you. It will make you feel good. You'll feel godlike. You'll feel free and empowered, and everyone will desire you." Sound familiar? Some of us have heard it directly or we have watched others we loved be taken in by this type of deception—a parent, a spouse, a sibling or child. We may not have realized that God experienced that when the devil came and stole his children, Adam and Eve, and the future human race, away from him. Satan stripped them of their innocence, violated their minds and crushed their souls (Genesis 3:22). We think God can't know what we're going through. But he does know how it feels. He knows all too well what it's like to lose a child to drugs, to lust, to murder, to suicide, to prostitution, to all the many pains of this world—to sin (Isaiah 40:27–28), and it pains him. It pained him so greatly he stepped down from heaven, bore himself through the womb of a willing handmaiden, experienced testing and temptations, taught many the ways of the kingdom, and suffered and sacrificed himself on our behalf.

God loves us so much he knows what is better for us than we do for ourselves. He knows the schemes of the enemy, and he knows the weakness of the human flesh. Satan and his demons were God's creation and belonged to him too but because of pride and rebellion lost their place with him in eternity. The Word of God says that he knew us before he formed us in our mother's womb. Before we were born, he set us apart (Jeremiah 1:5). He protects us from ourselves and from the plans of the devil when he allows us to be held "captive" for a time. But even though we are seemingly captive for a moment, Christ died to give us victory in each and every circumstance, and he does not leave us alone in any circumstance. He never leaves our side (Matthew 28:20). It's when we are held captive that we tend to lean on God. We look to him because he has our attention, and we are in a place to finally listen. We are more open to learn because frankly we don't like where we are at and we can't save ourselves. It doesn't feel comfortable. But the discomfort is for a moment because it's in that discomfort we learn to allow him to change our attitudes, our minds, our behaviors, and our lives. We begin to learn more about his character and his ways, and yes, while in captivity, we begin to learn about our enemy. It's important to know the characteristic of our enemy, Satan, as well. When we know how he works, we are equipped with wisdom and knowledge from on high to resist the devil's already defeated attempts to conquer us and to put our trust in God.

When we allow God to teach us, to shape us, to mold us, and we succumb to his ways and seek his understanding, we then *experience* the freedom he died to give us, that we would no longer be held captive by any mindset or sin pattern that keeps us in eternal captivity in this life. He does it for our own good. We get pressed, and we are shaped and molded, like the clay pot in the potter's hand (Isaiah 64:8). No two handmade pots are alike. One line or slight imperfection in one is different in another, yet each slight imperfection is what makes it unique—what gives it its beauty. It's the same when God does a work in us. None of us are exactly alike. We each have a treasure, a beauty about us that makes us unique, and it's in God's hands that those hidden beauties and treasures begin to take form and come forth and shine his light. God gives breath, life to it.

"I will give them hearts that recognize me as the Lord. They will be my people, and I will be their God, for they will return to me wholeheartedly" (Jeremiah 24:7). God wants us to be 100 percent completely sold out for him. He wants willing vessels that line up with his heart, his mind. Many of us have one foot in him and one foot in the world. It's time for us to choose and to choose wisely. We need to decide whom we will serve; the God of this world, which is the devil, the God of ourselves, which leads to the devil, or even the God of money, if not in its proper place becomes rooted in the devil. Anything we exalt above God, anything we choose to put before him, including our own families, will lead us into the slavery of hell (Luke 14:25). Or will we choose the God of the heavens and the earth, the God who loved us so much, and saw immeasurable value in us? Will we choose the God who created us in his image, who came down and bought us back from the slavery of the devil with his own blood, so we could be with him forever?

"But the rotten figs," the Lord says, "I will treat them

like spoiled figs, too rotten to eat. I will make them an object of horror and evil to every nation on earth. They will be disgraced and mocked, taunted and cursed, wherever I send them. I will send war, famine, and disease until they have vanished from the land of Israel, which I gave them and their ancestors" (Jeremiah 24:8–10).

What do we do with rotten fruit? Some of us push it to the back of our refrigerator and forget about it, until it molds and stinks up everything else, and then we finally do something about it. Others just look at it, see that it's rotting, and toss it out immediately. Either way the end result is that it gets tossed out, thrown away, never to be used again.

We do this in our own households and in our churches when we ignore the sin and push it back and allow it to stink up the rest of the family, the rest of the body of Christ. Now everybody experiences the stink from one person's sin. And everyone suffers from the sin of that person. We think we are only hurting ourselves in the process when we continue in sin, but we fail to realize that what we do affects those who are around us and who love us. If you leave something rotting for too long, such as a piece of fruit in a fruit basket, the fungus will transfer onto the good fruits and infect them with the disease. If you see what's happening and catch it soon enough, you can remove the rotting fruit and then cut away the beginning mold on the other pieces of fruit, and they can be spared (Matthew 12:33).

Sometimes we have to deal with sin in tough love. We don't want to, but we know it's the best way to save the person we love from continuous harm to themselves and continuous harm to everyone one else around them. We need to hold one another accountable (Hebrews 4:13, 13:17). We need to stop tolerating sin and looking the other way. I'm not saying treat the sinner badly. We are to hate sin but love the sinner. But we are also not to look the other way or make excuses for continual sin patterns. If we do, we give a foothold to the devil and keep the door open to the enemy of our souls to come into our homes, our sanctuaries, and corrupt the hearts of men. God is calling us to account, and he will convict our hearts, desiring our repentance that we may receive his gift of forgiveness.

God makes it very clear in Scripture that he is not only a loving God, but he is a God who hates sin (Genesis 6:5–7). He is separating the wheat from the chaff. No more passivity, laziness, being double minded, or willful disobedience. The time is short, and God is calling for those that are truly sold out for his will—those that want to partake in the kingdom movement of this end-time hour. It's time to advance, saints! We can choose to ignore the sin in our lives and in our congregations and push it back until it becomes so stinky and begins to stench up everything around us, or we get rid of it immediately by renouncing it, repenting, and allowing God to do the work in us and through us by surrendering our own agendas and our own motives. For those that don't want to allow God to get rid of their sin, for those that don't want to receive his love, his forgiveness, who are hardened in their hearts because of pride and rebellion, will ultimately get tossed out. God will cast those who want to remain in their sin and not receive his forgiveness to hell with Satan and his demons (Isaiah 65:12, Lamentations 1:8). This is no joke. There will be no other opportunities. When it's done, it's done. It can't be changed.

You see, in tough love, God's tough love, those "captive moments" become turning points in our lives. They become opportunities to change our direction, our ways, and deepen our relationship with the Father. Those captive moments often protect us from turning into rotting, stinky fruit that will eventually get thrown away. God loves you so much he wants to spare you from that fate. He desires that you would be examples of the fruits of his spirit—love, joy, peace, patience, kindness, goodness, faithfulness, gentleness and self-control (Galatians 5:22–23). But those that continue in their evil, their sin, their worldly ways, will be thrown out along with the rest of the world—an eternal consequence.

Discipline in love is the best love you will ever receive; when you receive that you experience true love (Job 5:17). Because the God of true love, unceasing love, wants the very best for you for his purposes, and the very best for you is himself. Surrender yourself to your loving Father's hands, and he will fashion you into that vessel of honor for his glory. "For I know the plans I have for you," says the Lord, "plans to prosper you and not to harm you, plans to give you a hope and a future" (Jeremiah 29:11).

Obedience is the Key to your Future

Queen Vashti was described as a very beautiful woman. But she was outcast because her pride, her thoughts, and attitude got in the way. She denied her king's request, so she was removed as queen. Simply put, she thought her way was better. Maybe she didn't want other men gazing at her beauty, but the king wanted to "show off" his bride, his queen. No matter what she thought at the time was right or wrong or better for herself, she decided to disobey the king, therefore refusing to honor him. *Honor* means "to esteem or regard highly." Since she refused to honor him, he didn't honor her, and she was removed as his queen (Esther 1:10–20).

Sometimes we don't want to honor our leaders or those God has set above us, and we don't want to bless them because we don't think they really deserve it. Yet we are commanded by God's two greatest commandments to love God and love others as you would love yourself. Sometimes God calls us to honor others whether we think they deserve it or not. The Word of God asks what we have to gain by loving those that already love us. No, it's when we honor, when we love those who are our enemies that we possess kingdom quality and attributes. It comes down to sacrifice and surrender. Do you sacrifice your own desires and surrender your own pride to honor those who have hurt you or have not measured up in your eyes? If you do, your Father in heaven will honor you. In turn, those who were once not your favorites may become your biggest allies. One act of obedience can turn a life or many lives around.

Now Esther was obedient and followed direction precisely. She was a simple girl but sincere, ready, willing to learn, and allowed herself to be led. She allowed herself to be prepared, to be bathed in pleasing oils and fragrance. She allowed herself to be dressed in royal garments and adorned with sparkling jewels that would captivate the attention of the king, her groom (Esther 2:15–19). At the time she didn't really know what she was truly being prepared for, but we see God had a plan and a purpose. There is a plan and purpose to everything that God does. He wastes nothing. A spiritual mentor and friend in the Lord once said something I'll never forget. He basically said, "While we are busy whining to God about why the plans for our lives aren't all taken care of or all our desires met, God is busy lining up the entire planet around his plans for your life." It's not just about us. It's about every other person on the planet whom you will either come into contact with or connect with that will come into contact with someone else, etc.

Imagine a God who has all of that in the palm of his hands. God is working on something particular in us that we may impact the world one life at a time for his glory. While you are waiting for that financial breakthrough, God is lining up and preparing that person from another town, city, state, or even country to receive their blessing. Then he's waiting for them to decide to become obedient and maybe catch that flight out for a conference in your state, the same conference that God blessed you to go to through a neighbor because you wanted to see the presenter. Then *bam,* you ended up in the very seat next to that person at the right time. All of this so God could prompt their heart to give you the financial blessing, an encouraging word, a job opportunity, or a partnership to help your own business reach even further. God works in amazing ways even in times we think we were late or we got mad because our flight was delayed, etc. He times it just perfect, and we never know until we see the end result. We then look back and go "aha!"

Divine appointments are what we often refer to them. The dictionary describes the word *divine* as "relating to or proceeding directly from God, superb, heavenly." Now that's a pretty awesome appointment. I don't know about you, but I wish all appointments in our lives were divine, and they could be. Your ordinary dentist appointment can lead someone to Christ, or a play date can turn into a word of encouragement for a mother who is hurting or struggling that day. A trip to the grocery store can turn into a provision for someone short money for their groceries in the checkout line. All they have in their cart is bananas and some milk, while the kids are crying and asking for some cookies. Have you been on the other end of any of this? Have you been hurting or been desperate for a divine appointment from God? Desperate for a moment when God steps into the natural and interrupts the circumstances by using someone to bless you at the moment you need it most? Imagine if someone doesn't step up to the plate. Maybe God called someone to bless you in that grocery line; but they were embarrassed of what you would think of them or that you might refuse their offer of generosity. Then they wonder what the other people in line would think of them. If you've experienced the need for a divine appointment, then you know how important it is to *respond* to a divine appointment.

God will take our obedience to bless us, or he'll take our *dis*obedience to bless someone else. If you don't want what God has for you, he will give it to someone else. He will raise up another who will hop on board his kingdom train and be willing to take on that ministry he wants birthed to bless many lives. Or bless that person who will step out in faith and lay hands on that cancer patient and command that spirit of infirmity to leave and the healing power of the Holy Spirit to take over.

I don't believe that Esther really had any idea what she was getting into at first. She didn't know the plan or understand the purpose yet; however, she stepped out in faith and trusted those appointed as leadership above her and became obedient. The obedience of this one woman changed the plans of the enemy and set free the Jewish nation that was destined for destruction. God chose a young servant girl to rescue his people from Satan's plans for them. If you don't know by now, you should; God is not a respecter of persons. He will choose any willing heart and obedient person who says, "Lord, send me for your purposes, not mine." Do you want to *be* a blessing? We need to change our focus from receiving a blessing to *being* a blessing. It's not wrong to want blessings from God, but when we understand that we receive blessings from *being* a blessing, we unlock wisdom and a kingdom mindset. We all need blessings from our heavenly Father, but they happen because God put it into the heart of a willing and obedient servant. He does it so we may be God's answer for the person needing a divine intervention.

When we obey, we not only help those we come into contact with, but we bring great joy to God's heart. Our focus should be how we can be a blessing to the Lord and his miracle to those he loves. God loves to bless his children, and it pleases him even more to bless them when they are obedient and willing to *become* the blessing. Now this is not to get you into a performance mindset. This statement isn't to cause you to run out and start giving all your money away to feed every person you see on the street and then expect God to pour out immediately a massive financial blessing. If he's leading you to do this well, then I'd say go for it. But be sure it's his voice. Most often, though, God puts it in your heart, and he tells you what he wants done and how he wants it done. Then you move forward on those specific instructions. Sometimes we tend to get overzealous and we jump ahead of God. Here me again; I'm not saying that it's not good to give, but be wise, give where God leads your heart. I'm not talking just about giving financially. I'm referring to giving your time, compassion, gentle pat on the back, a prayer, a word of encouragement, or whatever God is leading you to give of him. We need to follow his leading, or we can allow the enemy to slip in and deceive us. One of the enemy's tactics is to cause you to get ahead of God, to tell you, "No, don't wait. You deserve this now, and you've done what God has required of you. You should have this blessing now, so go out and get it. It's perfectly okay."

Well two things can happen. You can miss out on what God has for you altogether because you got ahead of him, or you've just settled for something less than what God has planned for you because you didn't wait for his perfect timing and receive what *he* wants to give you or someone else. What he wants to give us far surpasses anything we could hope for ourselves. God's ways are higher; his thinking is bigger. He sees the grand picture. He has great things set side for every one of us, but he will release it when he decides it's time. If we wait for him, we will be blessed beyond what we could have ever hoped or expected because God is a good giver. He is a giver of the finest.

Our obedience is also key to the blessings and futures of those around us: our families, unsaved loved ones, friends, coworkers. Again, it's never just about us. Everything God does in us impacts the lives of others. He prepares us to *be* the blessing to others, and he prepares their hearts to receive us as his blessing.

The Lord is fashioning a new bride. He's looking for believers that are willing, submitted, and obedient to make up this new bride. He's looking for believers who would display his splendor to draw the attention of others, believers who would draw those that are in the dark over to the truth and the light.

We can use Queen Vashti as an example of the *disobedient* bride of Christ. Queen Vashti didn't want to submit to her king's request and draw the gaze of others that day. There are many in the church that want the titles, the garments, and the honor but don't want to submit to the requests of the Lord. They don't want the Holy Spirit messing up their man-made programs and assemblies. Or they want to sneak in and do the "church thing" for their own conscience and sneak back out so they don't have to impact anyone. They don't stop and selflessly ask, "What can we do to please you, Lord?" or "How do you want to move in this service?" Like King Xerxes summoned Queen Vashti, Jesus has been calling for his bride, and she has been refusing his call.

But Esther's response was different. She served her king. She prepared a banquet for him (Esther 5:1–7). She willingly submitted to the leading and teaching of those who already knew the king well. She dared to approach the king, not in arrogance because she carried the title of queen, but in humbleness. She came dressed in royal garments of respect and honor and bore the fragrance of humility and gentleness. The king was so pleased that he let her come near to him to present her request and told her she could ask for anything up to half of the kingdom! Yes, he said half of the kingdom for her. *Wow!* But what did she request from him instead? Esther could have requested anything from him, but she requested his *presence*. She served *him* first, desired to bless *him* first. He was so moved and pleased by this banquet she prepared because she honored him. So he told her again to ask anything she wished and it would be granted. And again she asked for his *presence*. Now here we see that Esther asked for the king's presence not once but twice before she made her desires known, before she made her request to the king to move on her behalf. Many times we come to the Lord desiring from him. It's not wrong, but it pleases the Lord when we desire his presence first and we desire to honor him first before we think of ourselves. It's in the Lord's presence that we get to know him. It's in his presence that he reveals his desires, his mind, and his heart to us. It's in his presence that our desires begin to align and become one with his. Esther desired to get to know her king, to honor him that she would capture his attention and captivate his heart, ultimately receiving *his* honor and *his* favor.

These are the characteristics of the believers that will change the face of the church. Esther was a humble, willing, obedient servant. She was a bride who gave honor to her king, a bride that God is calling every one of us to be.

One person's choice to be disobedient caused death for all mankind, while another's obedience preserved the life of all mankind for those who believe.

The Esthers must arise in this eleventh hour, for at midnight our bridegroom returns for us. He will be looking for a bride that honors him, aligns with his desires, and reflects his glory, a bride that radiates his light so brightly that no darkness can withstand her brilliance.

Let the Worship Arise

In February 2007, the Lord gave me a dream. In this dream I was in the upstairs portion of the house I grew up in with my family members, and suddenly there were news reports on the TV that demons were invading homes. I looked outside, and I saw legions—and I mean legions— of demons with all different looks and sizes going inside people's homes looking for those they could imprison. In the neighborhood there is a park that runs down the middle of it, and you can get to all the different courts or streets on foot. I saw many demons patrolling those areas. I got my family out through a back window, and we hid in some shrubs while demons entered the house looking for people. As we hid, I saw demons of different ranks patrolling and on the lookout for "escapees." Secretly we went from shrub to shrub. Interesting enough, I was not afraid yet my heart beat like crazy because it was exhausting sneaking around trying to prevent from being seen. Surprisingly, I did not feel inclined at any time to stand in front of the demon hordes and bind and rebuke them, and I didn't know why. We went to friend's houses that lived in the neighborhood to attempt to rescue them, and I could see demons ransacking the houses and taking prisoners. We continued down the greenbelt as I was quickly trying to get my family members to the church in the neighborhood cul-de-sac. I saw many running into the church, and we had to move quickly as the enemy troops were on to the fact that many were seeking refuge there. We had to be quite sneaky and timely. Quickly I got my family inside the church. Many demons with spears were guarding and posting themselves around the outside of the church grounds, though they could not enter in, for it was holy ground. As I looked at the faces of those in the church, including the pastor, I saw the look of fear on their faces. They were completely frozen. I told them, "Use your authority, use your authority." Even the pastor looked helpless. Needless to say I was incredibly concerned as the demon hordes were taking over the whole neighborhood, and I got the impression the entire city as well. I left to search for others to help them inside the church, but the demons were coming after me. Just as one almost got to me, a car sped up with three people in the vehicle and told me to hurry and get in. I had no idea who they were at the time, but I just jumped in unafraid. I have a clue, though, that it may have been representation of the holy trinity. We then sped off toward a different direction toward more chaos to look for more people that we could help. Then I woke up.

As you can imagine, this was quite a puzzling dream until the Lord showed me something very key. I was confused about why the church was not using their authority and why their faces were in such fear. I'll never forget the look of the pastor who looked completely helpless as they cried out to the Lord for deliverance. They looked so desperate. Though they seemed to be safe inside the church walls, they were actually trapped there while the enemy was able to run rampant and take over the ground outside. The Lord explained to me that the reason why the demons were able to stick around and continue to rob and ransack and take unwitting (unsuspecting, unaware, accidental) hostages was because no one was praising, no one was worshipping!

There is coming a time, and I believe from the things God has been revealing that day is upon us, where enemy hordes in greater measures will be coming against cities, regions, and countries capturing the unsuspecting and attempting to create greater fear in the churches. Though in my dream the demons were not able to enter the church, they were able to stand outside and hold those captive *inside* the church building helpless. Much of the church has been unable to move. They've stayed inside their four walls, some rendered unable to step out because of fear and some because they are unwilling to get out of their comfort zones. A spirit of passivity to the enemy has fallen upon the unsuspecting. Worship will be the most truly effective weapon that is going to work against the enemy during the coming days. God's Word says he inhabits the praise of his people. There is a deep place of intimacy in the holy of holies where the enemy is not allowed to enter in with God's people. When I say worship, I specifically mean singing, dancing, and playing instruments (or pots and pans), although there are many other forms of worshipping God. Often we hold back or we take the worship part of service lightly or worry how silly we think we might look to others. I know in the beginning of my walk when I saw others raising their hands and swinging their arms during worship I got very embarrassed. But as I began to pursue more of God's presence and I began to pursue in Christ more revelatory knowledge and wisdom of heaven, I began to get to know my Creator in greater ways. I fell deeper in love with my Creator by getting to know him, by experiencing him, and resting and waiting in his presence. I began to *want* to worship him. As I pushed past my flesh and my embarrassment, I began to really offer up extravagant praises to my beloved Jesus. He deserves our praises and our worship. He deserves all that we are. He alone deserves that we would love him so deeply it would move us into that place of serenading our beloved and cascading him with a fragrant blanket of praise. When he hears that heart of worship, he is moved by the love, by the adoration of his people. Who wouldn't be? God is no different in that he desires to be loved and adored by the ones he calls his very own. "Love the LORD your God with all your heart and with all your soul and with all your strength" (Deuteronomy 6:5).

When we worship in complete abandon to the one who created us, who first loved us, no demon in hell can come against that. No attempt of the enemy can prevail. "The enemy prowls around like a roaring lion seeking someone to devour" (1 Peter 5:8). I guarantee, better yet God guarantees, when you worship the Lord, the enemy will not be able to devour you. The enemy is seeking to devour and to destroy God's people and their ministries. He seeks to devour the destinies of those called and even the next generation before they are born. He is seeking to devour families, marriages, schools, neighborhoods, towns, cities, and countries. His mission is to destroy the move of God by paralyzing the people. If we are paralyzed with fear, with stress, with worry, with depression, complacency, and self-pity, we will not praise, we will not worship and therefore will not invite heaven to earth. It is by our worship that heaven rips open and moves in physical manifestations and miracle-working power. It is by praise that the very presence of God rains down and transforms our hearts and circumstances.

If praise wasn't important, then why does God have specific angels praising him nonstop at his throne? "Each of the four living creatures had six wings and was covered with eyes all around, even under his wings. Day and night they never stop saying: 'Holy, holy, holy is the Lord God Almighty, who was, and is, and is to come'" (Revelations 4:8).

If praise and worship weren't important, how come David was considered by God a man after his own heart? David was a worshipper of God. David was also a victorious leader and a very prosperous king. Don't you find it interesting that he accomplished great things not because of his own strength but because he had heart of worship for God? David danced and leapt around his palace. "David, wearing a linen ephod, danced before the LORD with all his might" (2 Samuel 6:14).

Back in those days palaces had a lot of open-air construction and design, so I am sure many of his guards and servants saw him dancing before the Lord, praising his name. We know from the Bible that even one of his wives, Michal, saw him and was actually disgusted with his behavior because she didn't think it proper for someone of his stature, of his rank, to be leaping around like that. So if David, a mighty king, and a well-known, accomplished warrior could care less what others thought of him and danced before God, why can't we? We have no excuse not to be wholehearted worshippers of God. Yes, many will argue that everyone is different; we all worship differently. And yes, they are right to some aspect, some of us can sing better, some of us can dance better, some of us can play an instrument, but God doesn't care who can do better or who is more gifted. He looks at the heart not the tone deaf. His word says make a joyful noise (sound, racket, blast). Make an outward expression! In the wild, many species are drawn to one another because of the displays to show their desire for one another. Don't be content with staying where you are at with your worship. Go outside your own personal walls and take it up a notch. Show the Lord how very much you desire him. God is moved, and heaven is stirred by the heart of the people praising him. Don't hold it in and hold it back because of what others would think. Let what's in your heart explode for your heavenly Father. We should ask ourselves how come we can dance and jump and shout at wedding receptions, but we can't do the same for our beloved Jesus in anticipation of the wedding of the Lamb? There have been many conferences where people have been covered in gold and sapphire dust during the glorious encounters of God's presence. They called out singing in praise, dancing and jumping up and down to the one, Jesus Christ, and heaven answered back in a physical manifestation. There were displays of radical worship in unity that stirred the heavens and brought forth from the spiritual realm to the natural realm. Our praises and our worship can shake loose treasures from the spirit realm to the natural. "Shout to the Lord all the earth break out in praise and sing for joy! Sing your praise to the Lord" (Psalm 98:4–8).

> In unison when the trumpeters and the singers were to make themselves heard with one voice to praise and to glorify the LORD, and when they lifted up their voice accompanied by trumpets and cymbals and instruments of music, and when they praised the LORD saying, "He indeed is good for His loving kindness is everlasting," then the house, the house of the LORD, was filled with a cloud."
>
> 2 Chronicles 5:13

When we worship, we get an answer; a response from heaven. When we join together in total abandonment of the self and worship with all our hearts, it stirs the heavens. We invite the presence of the Lord to be in our midst. His presence envelops and covers us like a cloud, and we are in a place where no demon likes to reside—in the dwelling place of the Lord. It's a place of refuge and protection from the onslaught of the enemy. "If you make the Most High your dwelling, even the LORD, who is my refuge, then no harm will befall you, no disaster will come near your tent. For he will command his angels concerning you to guard you in all your ways" (Psalm 91:9–10).

> Happy are those who hear the joyful call to worship, for they will walk in the light of your presence, Lord. They rejoice all day long in your wonderful reputation. They exult in your righteousness. You are their glorious strength; Our power is based on your favor.
>
> Psalm 89:15–18

Worship transforms your mourning into dancing. We will walk in the light of God's presence as we worship. Imagine if the church through storms and trials worshipped their Maker anyway as if they were already in their promised land celebrating the deliverance of their Lord. The demons would flee because they cannot stand against the light of God. The light of God exposes the darkness, and it cannot hide. The demons make their whole purpose to hide in the church. They know if they are exposed they will have to flee. Often they mask themselves as religious spirits. Their plan is to deceive and to conceal any truth. They plan to paralyze the church to keep them from truly worshipping God. Worship is dangerous to their agenda. Satan knows this. If he can keep you down, he can keep you from worshipping. If the worship of the church brings the presence of God's light, then others would be drawn in. Like a beacon in the storm of this dark world, the church would be the salt and the light (the light of God's presence) of the earth. By nature we are attracted to light. Light gets noticed, and it commands attention!

Light awakens those who slumber and as the light of morning brings a new day it brings with it a new hope. With worship come answers from heaven, and brings with it deliverance. Remember while the disciples were in jail being held captive? They decided not to grumble, whine, or have self-pity; instead they praised their Maker. And when their singing was heard in heavenly realms, the Lord broke open the jail cells, and they were set free.

> About midnight Paul and Silas were praying and singing hymns to God, and the other prisoners were listening to them. Suddenly there was such a violent earthquake that the foundations of the prison were shaken. At once all the prison doors flew open, and everybody's chains came loose.
>
> Acts 16:25–26

"At the morning watch, the LORD looked down on the army of the Egyptians through the pillar of fire and cloud and brought the army of the Egyptians into confusion" (Exodus 14:24). Worship brings confusion to our enemies. Imagine in battle one team is attacking another; and they are feeling confident. To the natural eye it looks pretty evident that they are conquering the other team. But then despite what it looks like, the team that *appears* to be losing suddenly begins singing songs of joy and thanksgiving. Now tell me that it wouldn't confuse the heck out of you! Why are they praising when they are surely outnumbered? It causes the enemy to think there must be something they don't know or something must be hidden from them for these people to be joyful even though it looks as if they are losing the battle. That's what happened with Gideon and his army. They were severely outnumbered, and they defied all earthly logic to come against such a large troop of men. Yet because they used their trumpets of worship, it sounded as if there were many more than what they had. "When the three hundred trumpets sounded, the LORD caused the men throughout the camp to turn on each other with their swords. The army fled to Beth Shittah toward Zererah as far as the border of Abel Meholah near Tabbath" (Judges 7:22). I believe in my heart, though Gideon may not have known it at the time or maybe he did, that God released a legion of angels to sound trumpets along with Gideon and his small army. We aren't always aware what unseen forces are standing around us. Wherever we go and whatever we do, when in intimate relationship with Christ, we bring heaven with us.

Another example is Elisha's servant. He was afraid until Elisha asked God to open his servant's spiritual eyes. When God did, the servant could see that there were many more for him than were against him. "And Elisha prayed, 'O LORD, open his eyes so he may see.' Then the LORD opened the servant's eyes, and he looked and saw the hills full of horses and chariots of fire all around Elisha" (2 Kings 7:16). If we could praise with that kind of confidence every time no matter what our circumstances look like, then heaven would be ripped back, and there would be such an explosion of the move of God. How can God not move on behalf of such praise? Not only that but when we worship the scales from our eyes are removed, and we too can see with godly vision, wisdom, and understanding.

"He spoke to them in the pillar of cloud" (Psalm 99:7). God moves on behalf of the praises of his people! When we praise we tear down the unbelief in our lives, and then heaven moves into action in response to that heartfelt worship. We hear God more clearly when we are in the midst of his presence, his cloud. We build a godly confidence knowing who he is and clearly what he is directing us to do when we are in the midst of worship. There is clarity. In those deep intimate places of worship, God often shows us and tells us many things.

When David danced before the Lord in a linen ephod, it showed his transparency, his humility, his willingness to become a fool for God. He didn't come clothed in a majestic robe adorned with jewels. He came in simplicity but with a desire in his heart to love on his heavenly Father. He chose to give a great display that the Lord may see how very much he loved him. David wanted to move the very heart of God. The Lord won't love you less if you don't worship him in total abandon of the self. You won't even lose his favor or his protection over your life. God loves you exactly the way you are, and you don't have to perform for what you've already been given through Christ's death. But you will not *gain* the incredible beauty and consuming presence of him. You will not gain the abundant love *for* him that you will experience from worshipping Jesus the way he truly deserves to be worshipped, with your whole self. Ask God for a heart of worship for him; you'll be glad you did. And let your worship arise!

Glory and the Greater Glory

Often we think when we do the great things in God, when we have the greatest triumphs, and when we attain another spiritual level, we glorify his name. We think when we have victory over our tongue, we can speak in other languages and we increase in visions and dreams and receive a prophetic mantle that we will bring glory to our Father in heaven. When we get to that mountain top, then I've made it and God was glorified! This is all wonderful, but if we think it's only in these ways when we are on the mountain peaks that God is glorified then we have robbed ourselves of the experience and our Lord the demonstration of his *greater* glory in our lives.

When Peter stepped out of the boat and walked on water, God was glorified. But when Peter, in his human weakness, took his focus off the Lord and put his attention on the storm around him, he sank. Jesus did not let him drown. He did not stand idly by and say, "Bummer, Peter, you should have believed me; now look what happened." Jesus immediately reached his hand down and rescued Peter (Matthew 14:31–32). Yes, the scriptures say that Jesus spoke to Peter and said, "You of little faith, why did you doubt?" But Jesus wasn't asking the question of Peter to find out the answer. Jesus already knew the answer. He wanted Peter to discover the answer. Jesus already knew that Peter would step out of the boat. He knew he would take his eyes off his Lord, and he knew Peter would sink. Nothing came as a surprise for Jesus. He knew he would reach down and rescue Peter. By revelation of the Holy Spirit, I don't believe for one minute Jesus was chastising Peter for doubting, because he knew Peter would doubt. Jesus was aware of what Peter was made of—flesh. But the real question is did Peter know what he was made of? To back this up, we know God's Word says, " … I tell you the truth, if you have faith as small as a mustard seed, you can say to this mountain, 'Move from here to there' and it will move. Nothing will be impossible for you."(Matthew 17:20). The scripture doesn't say if you have *all* the faith in the heavens and in the earth then the mountain or circumstance will be removed. It says *as small* as a mustard seed. The glory was that Peter walked on water and that he stepped out in the level of faith he had at the time to walk toward his Messiah. The greater glory was that Jesus not only met him there but provided for Peter what Peter could not provide for himself—salvation!

Jesus saved Peter from death. By referring to Peter as *you of little faith*, he was reminding Peter that in himself, in his flesh, he could do nothing but with Christ all things were possible. When we compare God's level of faith to ours, we will discover ours is little. When Jesus asked Peter, "Why did you doubt?" he was merely showing Peter that there would be doubt when he was relying on himself and relying on his own faith in who he thought Messiah to be. But Jesus was teaching Peter about whom Messiah really was. He was building in Peter an understanding, a revelation of Christ as an image of the Father. Peter was on his mountain top while he was walking on water, but it was in his valley, when he sank, that Peter came to experience who Jesus really is. The Lord orchestrated it not just to be glorified but to be *greatly* glorified!

How else do we think we can gain revelation of who Jesus is? It is not merely by reading the word of God. Anyone can do that and never truly meet Jesus. There are those who can quote Scripture backward and forward yet still live completely defeated and void of all joy. It is by *experiencing* the word of God. It is transferring head knowledge of the word of God to root into the heart and become one with your spirit. God's word says "… write my laws upon your heart…" (Hebrews 8:10, 10:16). The Lord doesn't just want to be head knowledge; he wants to be revelation to the heart and to the spirit as well. When we experience the word, we desire to know Christ intimately, and that brings him *greater* glory.

There was a woman who was accused of adultery, was chased and fell onto the ground near Jesus. As the people were going to stone her, Jesus wrote in the ground and said, "… if any one of you is without sin, let him be the first to throw a stone at her." (John 8:7). They dropped their stones and left, and she was spared her original fate.

That brought God glory. Then Jesus said to her, "Where are your accusers? Did not even one condemn you? The woman responded "No." Then Jesus said to her "Neither do I. Go and sin no more" (John 8:10–12). The woman *experienced* the Lord's mercy by coming into the *revelation* of Christ's character through the mercy he had shown her. This brought God *greater* glory!

There was another, the immoral woman that came and knelt behind Jesus and wept at his feet. She proceeded to wipe her tears from his feet with her hair. She gained the understanding and revelation of Christ. She came with a beautiful jar filled with the most expensive perfume ever made in that time period and anointed his feet with it (Luke 7:37–38). She spared no expense. She knew Jesus was worth more to her than any costly thing in this world. She had revelation in her heart of Jesus. She came to love on him, to adore him, and to humble herself before him. That brought to the Lord greater glory. When he loves us and moves on our behalf, it brings him glory. But like the immoral woman, when we search for ways to love on him and take the time to adorn him with our love, our praise, our thanksgiving, and humble ourselves, he receives *greater* glory!

Do you see? When Jesus spoke about doing greater things than he did, I believe by revelation one of those things that he was referring to was giving greater glory to the Father. Jesus in his persecution, death, and resurrection gave glory to the Father, but that we believed, received, and proceeded to walk *in* his resurrection power brings the Father greater glory. This is not minimizing Jesus' suffering, death, and resurrection by any means. What I am expressing here is that we bring God great glory because we received his redemption for us and we seek to know him more intimately. It's when we come into understanding and revelation of who he truly is and walk in it. God's Word even says obedience is better than sacrifice. I believe God said this so we would know that there was no greater sacrifice than the death of Jesus on the cross for us! He isn't looking for who will sacrifice the most. He sacrificed himself on our behalf. What he is asking from us is our obedience (agreement, respect, conformity) to him. When we are in agreement to his direction, we display our love for our Creator. Now in our obedience we may end up having to sacrifice our fleshly desires at times but there is nothing greater than what Jesus sacrificed. The ultimate sacrifice was made, and our part is to be in agreement with him that we may display the very characteristics of Christ in our everyday journey. Knowing we are made in his image gives him glory, but when we choose to conform to his image that others may see his existence in us we bring him the *greater* glory.

What is this greater glory I'm talking about? In Acts 2 the tongues of fire fell, and the disciples were filled with the glorious presence of the Lord, baptized in the spirit, speaking other languages. People were being prayed for and healed, but if you look at Acts 4, you will see greater glory of the empowering of the Holy Spirit, an increase to include greater signs, wonders, and miracles. In Acts 4 we see that healings happened just by the shadow of a disciple. Acts 2 was just the tip of the iceberg as it increased the hunger and appetite for more of Jesus and for greater understanding and power from the kingdom. The ministry of Jesus encompassed so many valuable lessons for us, and one of those was an example about the difference between the glory and the greater glory. Our faith is activated in the glory, but it's in the greater glory that *his* faith takes over.

I once heard a minister of the glory give testimony that while being used by God to operate in this realm he told God, "I don't have the faith, Lord, for what you are asking me to do."

He said God immediately responded to him, saying, "It doesn't matter that you don't have the level of faith for this. I do"! From that moment on, he just did what God told him to do whether he had the faith for it or not.

We fail to realize that we are growing from glory to glory and building up our faith as we go along. We do this because we are still discovering more and more about our Lord as we experience him. God does not expect us to have a grandiose level of faith for what he's about to do; he expects us to allow him to reveal his level of faith to us. Often we put our faith in what God *does* instead of putting our faith in who God *is*. As most of us have experienced, God does things differently each time, yet he himself never changes. Our faith in him can only develop through intimacy. We need to take the time to seek his face, remain in his presence, because the more we allow him to reveal himself, his characteristics to us, the more we will grow in the faith he died to give us that we may operate in his image. How can we discover who God truly says he is if we do not experience him? It's in the valleys and the deserts that our faith grows and our intimacy with him deepens, not always on the mountain tops.

I was having a rough time one afternoon, and after calling out to the Lord, I called my best friend. When I heard her voice, I broke down crying and could hardly tell her what was going on. She listened to me express my emotions and let me just get in a good cry. By just listening and providing me with understanding, she brought the Father glory. But as I was speaking with her on her cell phone, my doorbell rang, and to my surprise she was standing at the door. She came to give me a hug so I would know how important I was to her and to Jesus at that moment. Then she proceeded to clean my kitchen for me, play with my children, and order dinner for me and my family that night so I wouldn't have to think about preparing a meal. That, my friends, brought the Father *greater* glory. I was not only blessed, but I experienced God's mercy, his compassion, his provision, and his love for me—all of this through one obedient heart, the heart of Christ living inside my best friend. I experienced first-hand who Jesus says he is through the love of another.

When we love him because he first loved us, it brings him glory, but that we love others as he loves us brings him *greater* glory (1 John 4:19). The Lord says the two greatest commands are to love God and to love others. He then says the second command is *greater* than the first.

Are you getting this now? Behold God is doing a new thing. Can you not see it? Can you not perceive it? (Isaiah 43:19) He is separating those that know *of* him from those that love him! Because those that *really* love him love others. By loving others, we exemplify (demonstrate, represent, epitomize, embody) who he is. When we exemplify who he is, then others will experience who the Father is through the love you show them. God gives to us that we may pour it out on others, not keep it for ourselves. We are commanded as true believers to share the good news, not just through the written or the spoken word but by the *living and active* word of God, the testimony of Jesus himself. Having faith brings God glory. Putting that faith into action so it can become experience and be written upon your heart and the hearts of others brings him *greater* glory (John 15:8). God doesn't just deserve to be glorified. He deserves to be greatly glorified!

> And I will harden the hearts of the Egyptians, and they will charge in after the Israelites. My great glory will be displayed through Pharaoh and his troops, his chariots, and his charioteers.
>
> Exodus 14:17

> Then the glory of the moon will wane, and the brightness of the sun will fade, for the Lord of Heaven's Armies will rule on Mount Zion. He will rule in great glory in Jerusalem, in the sight of all the leaders of his people.
>
> Isaiah 24:23

> The future glory of this Temple will be greater than its past glory, says the Lord of Heaven's Armies. And in this place I will bring peace. I, the Lord of Heaven's Armies, have spoken!
>
> Haggai 2:9

Then everyone will see the Son of Man coming on a cloud with power and great glory.

Luke 21:27

Shouldn't we expect far greater glory under the new way, now that the Holy Spirit is giving life?

2 Corinthians 3:8

All of this is for your benefit. And as God's grace reaches more and more people, there will be great thanksgiving, and God will receive more and more glory.

2 Corinthians 4:15

They wondered what time or situation the Spirit of Christ within them was talking about when he told them in advance about Christ's suffering and his great glory afterward.

1 Peter 1:11

Return to Bethlehem

As I was puttering around my house one day and thinking about the Christmas season, I suddenly became aware that I had been singing in my mind the song "O Come All Ye Faithful." But the first line really got me pondering. It starts out like this: "O come all ye faithful, joyful and triumphant, oh come ye, oh come ye, to Bethlehem."

As I really thought about that particular line in the song, I heard the Father speak to my heart and say, "Return to Bethlehem." It was then that the Lord showed me that this song was a song of remembrance for his faithful ones. In the song God is calling us his faithful. As his faithful he beckons us to come boldly full of joy and triumph back to Bethlehem. "O come ye" is mentioned twice because God is summoning us to Bethlehem. He desires us to return to and reflect upon Bethlehem, the place where hope was born and where hope was restored!

The times were very dark in Israel prior to the birth of Jesus. God's temple had been turned into a marketplace. Everything that was once considered holy and consecrated was no longer treated sacred. Sin had run rampant, and it seemed evil had prevalence; it had dominion. The enemy of our souls was claiming Israel as his territory. Those who believed in the Lord and were following him were in a place of disappointment and some in despair. I believe from what the Lord has been showing me they were in a place spiritually where some of us have found ourselves at times, in a place where hope was beginning to fade away as darkness seemed to take over even the faithful.

But it was in that very dark hour God had a plan. And where hopelessness prevailed, hope was restored. Jesus, the Messiah, the Savior of the world was born. Who would have thought a tiny little helpless baby would be the only hope mankind would need? God moved on behalf of the cry of his remnant for him to save them from the wickedness that surrounded them, from the poverty, illness, and famine that threatened their very lives, their very existence. Even though they couldn't see it, *hope* was growing inside a faithful woman for nine months. But hope was about to be birthed, and his name was Jesus.

Every year has many promises attached to it for God's remnant. When we think God hasn't answered our prayers you need to know that he has answered them the moment the prayer left our lips. We just couldn't see it growing inside of each and every one of us for a good portion of the year.

Many sacrifices were made prior to the birth of Jesus. Many were made in order to bring about the birth of Jesus. Just as Mary made many sacrifices and suffered persecution, hardship, fear of the unknown in order to bring about the promise for mankind, we too have suffered in our journey of faith for many others. We too have gone before and laid down our lives for the sake of encouragement and spiritual preservation for another. There are those that need what God has birthed inside of you. In order to birth, you must go through the preparation of that birth, some of it exciting and some of it very painful. But you can be used by God to restore hope to the hopeless and to encourage the discouraged, to ignite faith where faith did not exist. All this because you received the life that Jesus laid down for you, and so you have laid down your life for others. You may not see it or understand it yet but get ready. Continue to breathe, continue to wait, continue to trust, because God is about to birth something great through you that others are waiting for. It is a great privilege to be chosen to deliver hope into another who is suffering or even perishing. You have been chosen to know Jesus, to walk with Jesus, to share the life of Jesus with others. So when all seems bleak in your life right now, when hope has been lost and your faith has taken a beating, return to Bethlehem. Just like the three wise men, allow that bright star from heaven, the presence of God, to guide you through the darkness and lead you to your answer. And remember that when all seems lost, hope has been restored.

So now, "Come all ye faithful, joyful and triumphant, o come ye, o come ye to Bethlehem."

The Widow's Mite

And He sat down opposite the treasury, and began observing how the people were putting money into the treasury; and many rich people were putting in large sums. A poor widow came and put in two small copper coins, which amount to a cent. Calling His disciples to Him, He said to them, "Truly I say to you, this poor widow put in more than all the contributors to the treasury; for they all put in out of their surplus, but she, out of her poverty, put in all she owned, all she had to live on."

Mark 12:41–44

Have you ever felt as if you had nothing to give? Not even a penny to your name. Have your bank accounts been in overdraft, debt piling up, and you are borrowing from others just to have gas to get back and forth to your job? Has your phone continued to ring off of the hook daily reminding you of what you owe to your bill collectors?

Even if you haven't experienced this, I know at some point in all of our lives we experience a period of stretching in our finances and in ourselves—our heart, our mind, and our faith, instances when we feel as if everyone wants something from us like our money, our time, and our energy. We cannot give it because we frankly don't have it. It's not just that our bank accounts are overdrawn, but sometimes our love accounts and our spirits are in overdraft. There are days that there isn't anything left of you to give.

It is then that the enemy takes full advantage. I don't know about you, but I know I've had days when I cannot get my brain to function so I can form words or I can barely utter a word of thanksgiving. It is in this time we know we need to praise and worship, yet nothing comes out when the music plays or when you settle in to pray. I used to think maybe I was just rebelling against my heavenly Father and not giving him honor that was due. Or I believed I was being selfish and not giving God all my time and energy. That's what the enemy wanted me to think because soon afterward condemnation and guilt would come flying through the door of my mind. Or he would wrap me into a striving mentality that would leave me exhausted and disappointed at the lack of *my* expected outcome. It was just another attempt of Satan to pull me further from my Father's truth and into a dark pit of disappointment and self-pity. Oh how crafty Satan is even at masquerading as an angel of light. He enters in with religious undertones that "sound" like truth but they are just sugar-coated lies to alter your perception and cause you to question your worth and the Father's love for you.

When we hear the story of the widow's mite, we may automatically think of this story in monetary terms. I know I used to. But now I truly believe it's more than just that. It's a valuable lesson on giving, not just money, but giving your heart. Jesus wants your heart, not your money. But if money is currently where your heart is, giving that as he calls you to give it implies you are putting trust in him with what is precious to you. That act of faith is also an act of giving your heart. Some may not agree with what I am saying, and that is okay. I have learned that we don't all come into the kingdom dressed and ready to give our all and give up everything. It's a process that comes from building a relationship with Jesus. We may not always have our hearts in the right place, but we can *desire* to have our hearts in the right place and allow the Holy Spirit to line us up according to his ways. That is called surrender. We surrender our desires for his, and when we do that, we give him what is in our heart. "How can I know all the sins lurking in my heart? Cleanse me from these hidden faults" (Psalms 19:12).

Like the lesson of the widow's mite, there will be times in our spiritual journey when we have almost nothing to give—times where we are spiritually dried out and physically limited, when we are burned out in our minds and crushed in our hearts. But when we choose to turn to our heavenly Father during those times anyway, when we whisper a word of gratitude or lay prostrate before a worship song, we are giving a widow's mite. "Then call on me when you are in trouble, and I will rescue you, and you will give me glory" (Psalm 50:15). Jesus saw much more value in someone giving all that they had no matter how minimal it was than someone giving a little bit in their plenty. When all we can do is to give what we have left, *all* that we have, it is as if we have given him everything. It displays our trust and our love for him. Trusting him with all you have is invaluable to Jesus. "Wherever your treasure is, there the desires of your heart will also be" (Matthew 6:21).

Many of us have moments where we dance, worship, and praise and are feeling blessed and highly favored of the Lord. It's an amazing gift when we have days like that, but if we are honest, there are also days we don't *feel* any of that and we have no idea what is around the corner for us, days where we have taken hit after hit from the enemy through uncontrollable circumstances and our flesh has robbed us of all joy. Then we weep, we cry out to God and choose to believe him for the impossible. That, my friend, is your *widow's mite*. You have given to him all that you have. He receives it, and even though it is very little, he sees it as all the riches in the kingdom. Do you know why? It was because you chose to give it to *him*. You chose to cry to *him*. You chose to lie on the floor face down and wait for *him*. You chose to lift your eyes to *him* even if for a second or two. You chose *him*. His desire is for *you*…just as you are! We think sometimes, *Well I couldn't fast for three days straight* or *I didn't have three hours to worship or ten to read the Word.* Did you give him all you had to give at that moment? Did you give him yourself no matter what state you were in at the time? If you did then you gave him everything.

Now, I don't mean we should be lazy and give him a little bit of ourselves when we know we have more to offer. What I really mean is did you give him little because that is all you had? If it was, I'll say it again: you gave it all. Jesus received honor from it, just like the widow and her mite. We need to stop beating ourselves up, because frankly, we have a devil who runs around doing that. We need to stop making his job easier. If anything we need to make Satan's job harder. The more we condemn ourselves for not being a "perfect Christian," the more we open the door to defeat in our lives. Christ wants our hearts, and if we give him that no matter how little may be in our hearts at the time, it's as if we gave it all. It all comes down to you can't give what you don't have. If God wants more from you, he will put it in you to be able to push just a little harder. To God all that you have is more than enough for him. He can do so much more for you when you are fully dependant on him in every area of your life. Wherever you are lacking, his grace is sufficient. So when you can't even whisper a word of praise, just turn the worship music on and listen to it. Before you know it, you may be able to get a praise word or two in, and your offering will bless the very heart of God. Or maybe you won't, and at least your spirit will be built up by listening to the songs. God is not looking for the fanciest prayers, loudest worship, or daily fasts. He's looking for the fragrance of *your* widow's mite.

"Your love delights me, my treasure, my bride. Your love is better than wine, your perfume more fragrant than spices"(Song of Solomon 4:10).

The Remnant

There is a difference between knowing the will of God and doing the will of God. Though many of us claim to know the will of God; few of us follow in obedience to actually *do* the will of God. We are in a time when God is looking for those who will be *doers* of the Word of God not just *hearers*. What good is faith if it is not backed up with action? How can we claim we are in the will of God if we are not following his word, his command, his teaching? Sometimes it's hard to recognize that when we are not following his command, we are in disobedience. By failing to follow the word of God and apply it, we are actually in rebellion and disobedience. According to the word of God, rebellion and disobedience are sin in God's eyes (Psalm 106:43, Deuteronomy 28:15). God also says that obedience to his word, his command, is better than sacrificing something for him (1 Samuel 15:22). He'd rather that you give him your obedience than anything else. When he has your obedience, he has your heart and you are lining up your will with his will. His word also states that you "will reap what you sow." (Galatians 6:7) If you sow nothing in the spirit realm, you will reap nothing. God's people suffered often as a result of their disobedience to the Lord. He allowed their enemies to conquer their land, to enslave them and allowed famine and plague to befall them, again all results of their chosen disobedience. When we choose not to follow God's instructions, his word, we are in disobedience, and we allow open doors for our enemies to come and take from us all God had intended to prosper us spiritually and in the natural. I'm not talking about just material things. What we deposit in the spirit realm becomes our reality in the natural realm. Many people are prosperous on this earth, but it will all amount to nothing if they have not deposited anything into the spirit realm. But those that hear the word of the Lord and apply (use, operate, affect) will have a prosperity that will last for eternity.

> Do not store up for yourselves treasures on earth, where moth and rust destroy, and where thieves break in and steal. But store up for yourselves treasures in heaven, where moth and rust do not destroy, and where thieves do not break in and steal. For where your treasure is, there your heart will be also.
>
> Matthew 6:19–21

"If a man is lazy, the rafters sag (wilt, droop, drop), if his hands are idle (inactive, lazy, futile, empty), the house leaks (seep out, let slip, give away)" (Ecclesiastes 10:18, author paraphrased). Our rafters are our support beams to our roof. Our roof is our covering, and our authority as believers in Christ. If we are lazy in applying God's commands and his word, our support beams will begin to fall and so will our authority over the enemy. If we are inactive by hearing the word of God and then going about our own business in the world, everything we do becomes futile, or empty in God's eyes. Our houses, which are our dwelling and also our physical person, our temple, begin to leak out the anointing and glory that God has placed in us. I'm not referring to giving away what God has given you as a blessing; I'm referring to losing what he has placed in you when you become disobedient. Does God take it away from us? I don't believe he does. I believe we let it leak and we let it evaporate (fade away, dissolve, or soften) instead of taking what God has placed in us and becoming effective. Again God's Word says faith without works (labor, effort, effect, and drive) is dead (lifeless, obsolete, empty) (James 2:20, author paraphrased). Hear me now; this again is not a performance statement where you need to do all this "stuff" for God. He is not interested in all the stuff. He is interested in the heart of a man or woman that we would diligently follow after him, after his command—that we would be effective containers and givers of his light. I'm specifically talking about the faith in God that drives us to trust in his Word, apply it, and become effective sons and daughters of the kingdom of Christ.

"If the ax is dull and its edge unsharpened more strength is needed but skill will bring success" (Ecclesiastes 10:10). Let me ask, what good does it do your spirit man to go to a church service to listen to the Pastor and then do nothing with it? You cannot and you will not grow in the things of the Lord if you do not apply the teaching to your life. God's word creates. God spoke his word; and the heavens and the earth came into being, the sun and the moon and the stars shined, and the waters covered the earth and plants and animals were birthed—all of this through God's spoken word. That was an example of God's word in action! God's word wasn't just formed, but it was put into action and spoken. There is power and life in the spoken word of the Lord. One of the meanings of the word *speak* is to address (tackle, take in hand, take up, direct, deliver). When we put God's word into action, we *tackle* that awful circumstance, we *take in hand* the sword of the Lord, and we direct the supernatural to move on behalf of the natural, and *deliver* results and life into what we are doing.

We stand here breathing today because we are God's word in action. We need to partner with God. We can't just leave it to someone else like our pastors, our parents, or our spouses to be our faith in action. We need to represent the fullness of God's word ourselves. When we rely on others for our faith and for our own circumstances, we are being lazy. God wants us to take hold of our own futures by directing our destinies with his word, his instructions, not according to our own agendas and desires but according to the desires of the Father. We aren't to manipulate God's word for our own selfish gain. He has given every one of us a destiny. We just have to step into it. He has given us the tools, and we need to use them, exercise them. He didn't give them to us to have them sit upon a shelf and become dusty, rusty and dull. When we become idle and dull, the light of God dims in us. The enemy, Satan, sees this and uses this opportunity to pounce on us. Our light should shine so bright that the darkness would flee from our presence. This is not to say that the enemy will not try to come against you ever, but I believe the encounter will be briefer the brighter the light of God inside us. Some demons will not even bother because they know it is futile. It's all training. We are to use our spiritual tools so we become familiar with them and we become skilled in using and applying what God gives us. When we do this, our tools become sharpened. In example the more you speak the word of God, the quicker it will come to you and the sharper and more effective you'll be.

In the early part of 2007, the Lord gave me a dream. In this dream I was standing at the bottom of a large structure that was being built. I guess you would say I was at the foundation floor. There was a construction worker, the foreman specifically that was showing me the foundation and the structure of the building as it was being built up. I saw the cement footings and then huge steel bars. I also viewed the rebar where the cement walls were being built, and it looked like a rock-solid structure. I then looked and observed a multitude of crystal strings hanging down from heaven. There was no roof present because the structure was still in its building process. These crystal strings went up into the air seemingly without end, and I could not see where they attached. But as I looked I saw people of the Christian faith. They were familiar faces, like Joyce Meyer, Kim Clement, Matt Sorger, Paula White, Todd Bentley, and many other prominent and well-known forerunners for God. I noticed each of them holding onto a crystal string tightly. But they were not just hanging there. The weight of each individual was creating tension and pulling the string down, and then it would pull back up as a natural response to gravity and physics. I wasn't sure what I was witnessing at first. I looked again, and I saw many laborers, vineyard laborers walk down in dirty jeans and dusty white shirts and each grab a crystal string. Again I was puzzled as to what I was seeing. Then all of a sudden, I was taken to this mountain top, and standing next to me was the presence of someone in a white robe. Though I never looked at his face, I felt his strong presence there speaking to me inaudibly. As I looked down from the mountain top, I saw a beautiful valley and amazing sunset with purple mountains in the background that seemed to be surrounding the building structure. However, it looked different this time. Instead of the original building structure I had previewed, I now witnessed these crystal strings lined up together in various heights so that it made the outline of the most beautiful cathedral I had ever seen. *(Lord, give those who are reading this the vision that they may see it as I observed it. I pray in Jesus' name).*

From the mountain top, I could hear the sound of bells. It was so beautiful, and sounded exactly like wedding bells at a church. Then before I knew it I was at the bottom of the building structure again. I looked once more and saw that each person holding onto a crystal string was making a unique bell chime while holding onto their individual string. But when each individual chime joined together with the others it all came together in this beautifully melodic wedding bell-like song. There are not even earthly words to describe this amazing sound. As the dream continued, I saw a crystal string before me, so I stepped forward, climbed up it, and I took my position. Making my own unique sound as the string went up and down it felt as if I were riding a carousel horse. I had perceived in my spirit man that God was asking if I would step forward and become part of this remnant that he was calling me to. Then I awoke.

As I meditated on this dream and did a little research regarding some of the symbols, God gave me the interpretation. Crystal, I discovered in *The Prophets Dictionary* by Paula Price, symbolizes wisdom and spiritual revelation, and it is considered an incorruptible purity because of its transparent appearance. It is also considered a transmission (broadcast, communication, conduction) of the spiritual to the natural. The mountains surrounding the structure symbolized meetings of those on high powers and the center of a spiritual community. The Lord had taken me to the foundation of the structure and showed me what it was built on-the strong foundation of Christ. Then he took me to the mountain top to see his plans from his viewpoint. The man in the white robe was the Lord himself. The construction foreman was a representation of the Holy Spirit as he was explaining the structure and the plans to build up. The foundation of the building with the large cement footings and thick steel rods was a representation of Jesus . The vineyard laborers were explained by the Lord through his divine revelation as those who were unafraid to labor hard, to put their shoulders to the plow, and their nose to the grind. Specifically it represented the intercessors—those that labor on their knees in prayer day and night. God did not differentiate those who were in leadership or at the forefront from those that were laborers in his vineyard. All were given their own crystal string. Not one person was considered in God's eyes as above the other. Each person, according to their God-given gifts, made their own unique sound and impact, and it resonated throughout the heavenlies with such beauty. So much so that when joined together in unity and in harmony it created the most beautiful wedding bells.

God is speaking to his bride in this final hour. He is requiring our diligence, our obedience that he may use us according to what he created us for—his glory. He is separating the sheep from the sheep–believers that choose to follow him versus believers that choose to live according to their own plans. Those that are fully sold out for his passion and effective for his purposes are invited to take up their own crystal string and become his remnant, his true bride. With much that is given, much is required (Luke 12:48). So I pose this question to you today: Will you step up and take hold of your crystal string and become part of that remnant that God is calling to impact this world? There is a crystal string for everyone who wants to take part. God will not refuse those who will not refuse him.

Part Two

Revelation for your Mind

Let the Water Flow

Awhile back our one bath and shower stopped working correctly. We were getting hardly any water flow from the shower head, and the tub would fill up so fast you had to hurry before it flooded. The pressure of it all would cause the lever or stopper to automatically kick up and shut off thus creating the flood of water in the bathtub that would not drain. We might have become the family who held a record for the fastest shower in the west except it took forever to get the shampoo to rinse out. Finally enough was enough. We knew it should get fixed and work the way it was supposed to. So we called our landlord, since this was an old shower and if something broke we didn't want to be responsible as it was not our property. Fortunately he came out and fixed it. But in order for it to be fixed, he needed to break the old pieces of the faucet to get them off in order to replace them with the new. The corrosion over the years of water, soap, and just plain old age was enough to cause it to not function properly thus resulting in poor water flow and drainage. So with the new parts, I tried out the shower the next morning and wow! I mean, wow! It was water pressure like never before. The strong flow of water was so great, in fact, it had never worked that well ever; from the first day we moved in. I couldn't believe it. The bathtub didn't fill up to my mid calves; it drained properly. You barely turned the knobs, and the water would come on instead of having to crank it several times over to get the water out. Everything was working perfect and even beyond my expectation. In my mind I thought to myself, *This is one of the best showers I've had in a long time. I wonder why?* Only to have the Lord speak to my heart without missing a beat, *Because sometimes things need to break in order for the new to come and replace it.* Immediately my mind was flooded with greater understanding from the Lord.

The Minnesota-bridge catastrophe in August 2007 was very symbolic to the *spiritual* breaking of weak bridges and weak connections. I use this example only because of the revelation the Holy Spirit imparted to me through this tragic event, not to make light of the situation and the unfortunate parties involved. My heart goes out to the families of those who lost their lives as well as those who were injured physically and emotionally. I thank Jesus that there was not greater devastation. However, looking at this in a spiritual parallel, God desires to replace the weak bridges in our lives with new bridges and new connections, him being that new connection. Sometimes it takes a breaking for us to even recognize that there is anything even wrong with it in the first place. Often we don't recognize a weakness because we just drive over it or past it going about our business. Or we have this motto of "if it's not broken, don't try to fix it." Yet when we spot weakness or potential to form problems, we need to deal with it then and there, not wait until it breaks. But then there are those times we aren't fully aware of the corrosion lying underneath. It masks itself so well we don't recognize that it's not right or working to its full potential or working the way it was created to work. Then, something *has* to break—old habits, old patterns, old beliefs, old attitudes, old relationships. Sometimes the old must break in order for us to even embrace something new. Human nature is to just exist in the comfort zone of life, the old attitude of if it works, no matter if it's puttering or making noises, leave it alone. We spend a lifetime sweeping old hurts and pain and conflicts under the rug and never dealing with the issues at hand until something breaks, and sometimes that something is *us*. When something breaks then it grabs our attention. It needed our attention all along, but it's only when it has broken and becomes an inconvenience to us or those around us we are in a place where we suddenly have to deal with the issues at hand. It's not God's desire for things to have to break all the time in order to get our attention. But if we ignore the important things that need attention, corrosion can cause something to work improperly to the way it was designed and, like the shower, slow down the flow of the water. In our spiritual life, it's similar. When we choose to ignore the things that God is speaking to us or trying to gain our attention on, we can slow the flow of the Holy Spirit in our lives due to the corrosion of sin. When God is revealing a sin in our life, we need to allow God to make the changes necessary to rid ourselves of those habits. The Lord is a gentleman; he won't force us. It takes discipline sometimes to lay before the throne of God and allow him to purge us of impurities and fashion us after him. The fact is we can't do it on our own. He has to do it in us. But then there are moments the breaking comes as a result of us trying to protect others or even ourselves from truth that needs to be revealed. We can carry a fear of the unknown if the truth is revealed, and yet God's Word says, "Then you will know the truth, and the truth will set you free" (John 8:32). We want so badly to control the outcome of things. It's a natural instinct, self-preservation if you will. And yet the very things you are trying to protect others from including yourself may be the very things that the enemy uses to destroy lives.

Sometimes those bridges or walls of protection, a false protection, need to come down in order for bridges of healing and connection to a new path or a new direction can happen. His Word says that he "plans to prosper you and not to harm you, plans to give you hope and a future" (Jeremiah 29:11). It's the enemy that wants you to continue on a path that leads you in a way from truth and into a treacherous mountain of lies in which you feel there is no escape. But yet our Lord loves us so much that he allows a breaking down of things for our sake. The very thing that can make you feel uncertain, afraid, shaky, and the loss of control can be the very thing that sets you free and sets you up for God's best.

You must ask yourself some hard questions. Who is in control? We don't realize that when we attempt to protect ourselves or others often we are trying to control the outcome of something. There was a point in my life when I needed to release and expose something. Years of fearing the reactions of others and the fear of hurting others kept me bound. I reasoned it away so many times thinking, *Well, sometimes God will allow things to be kept secret.* I had even heard others in ministry say that sometimes it's not always best to rock the boat. But the truth was at least a few times a year a horrible anxiety would grip me. It would become so severe I would cry and cry when no one was around and I would want God to just take me from this earth so I didn't have to deal it. It was such an intense fear and anxiety I would actually feel horribly sick to my stomach; I couldn't breathe, and I wanted to run until I collapsed.

Feelings of anger, resentment, and rebellion would manifest in me. I felt alone in my pain as I had somewhat of a code of silence placed upon me. The silence was not written in the Word of God, but in the enemy's book of lies it was written that I needed to remain silent. Then after one of my anxiety episodes, I decided enough was enough. Just like the shower I spoke of earlier, *I* was not working the way I was intended to function, the way God created me. I knew Jesus died on the cross to set me free, not just from some things, but from *all* things. It was time to expose the enemy after over twenty years of feeling anguish, shame, and condemnation. I couldn't live like this anymore. God did not want me to live like this anymore. The bridge of guilt and shame I crossed over every day of my life needed to break. That wasn't the bridge Jesus built for me with his spilled blood, painful death, and beautiful, glorious resurrection. The bridge he built was one of freedom, grace, mercy, and his tender and jealous love for me. But in my despair and my feelings of being a victim, I had no idea I had inadvertently controlled the situation and helped Satan build my own prison. He said I had to keep quiet; God didn't. God never said that to me once. I said it to myself many times. Not wanting a possible "mess" on my hands, I bought the lies that Satan fed me, and I lived by them. Until the day I decided that's it; I'm done. I finally *wanted* the freedom Jesus paid for me more than the prison cell Satan helped me build. It was then that the Lord showed me a vision of a little Dutch boy with his finger in the dam. You may have heard the little fable in school. I knew immediately what the Lord was talking about. The little Dutch boy's finger was preventing the flow of the water from leaking from the wall of the dam. By doing this he was trying to keep the wall of the dam from crumbling and all the water flooding the village. The problem was once his finger was there he imprisoned himself to the chore of protecting everyone else in the village when he himself couldn't say for sure if the dam really would have broken. Like the little Dutch boy, the silence I maintained all those years imprisoned me, and I couldn't be free to be who I was intended to be. I was too busy protecting my "village" from a possible hurtful truth. But again, I didn't know for sure how it would turn out. I just continued to buy the lies and allow my imagination to run with all the reasons why it would be catastrophic if I did reveal the truth. But as the vision continued, the little Dutch boy, representing myself, stood there, and I heard God say to me, "Remove your finger." So I did. And in the vision, the dam did break, and the waters flowed. Most would think that was a bad thing, but from God's perspective, in the vision, many things happened. The wall of false protection crumbled, and the healing waters, the Holy Spirit of God, flooded that village and touched not just the little Dutch boy but every person in that village. God reminded me of the promise of salvation for all of my family members. In my quest to protect them from the truth, I very well could have been preventing the Holy Spirit from flowing through not only my life but through the lives of those I love. Because I chose to take my finger out of the dam and trust God with the outcome, I now have experienced my freedom, the very freedom Jesus paid a high price to give me. Freedom isn't free. It costs somebody something. Jesus paid that toll for me so I could cross the bridge of freedom into a deeper connection with my Lord and live a life worthy of his death for me. The healing is taking place as I am soaking in those waters that flooded the village of my life. But I am excited about the new bridges I get to cross, the connections to the abundant life Christ gave his life for me to have. I am excited to really begin to live in the freedom I was given long ago when two pieces of wood were connected together to hold the sacrificial, unconditional love of my Savior.

Are you that little Dutch boy with the finger in the dam trying to prevent the wall from coming down and the water from flooding your valley? If so, aren't you tired of trying to hold it all together? The very thing you are preventing could be the very thing that comes with God's power and blessing. God wants that dam to break because that wall has slowed or possibly even stopped the flow of his Spirit. When you remove your finger and the pressure of the powerful flow of the Holy Spirit presses on that unhealthy wall, it will crumble down, and that healing water will invade you and overtake you with all of God's goodness. Are we preventing his flow from entering the valley of our hearts? Remember he won't violate your free will. But from my own experience I encourage you to let go and allow God to overtake you and all those around you. You aren't responsible for the results; God is. He is faithful. He has it all under control even when we question the outcome.

That being said, God is releasing a breaker anointing upon his people in greater measure. Old ways of living need to fall away. The church as a whole is not reaching the lost and releasing the faithful followers with their blessings into greater territories with God as she was intended. This anointing that God is dispensing is breaking the ideology in the church, the things that are not working properly or working the way God created it to work in our churches, our marriages, and our lives. The flow of the Holy Spirit has been held back too long, and it's ready to come through not as a steady, predictable flow, but with *power*! He is breaking our way of living and replacing it with *his* way of living. The atmosphere of heaven is invading the earth. God is breaking bondages and strongholds, old mindsets, old strategies, and old religious attitudes. And it's coming like the crash of a wave. When the waves break onto the sand, you can almost feel the power. The sand is moved from its position and carried away by the water out into the ocean. God wants to carry his people away with the Holy Spirit. He is drawing us into *his* deep ocean, where we will be fully dependant upon him. We can no longer compromise and have dependence on anything else but him and him alone. Most of the Church has been existing without God forgetting that the Church was created to know God, to follow God, to be led by God, and to be one with God. We were created by him *for* him. We have separated ourselves from our one true love—some of us intentionally and some of us unintentionally. But God is drawing us into the deep ocean of himself, where we may discover the vastness of him, the beauty of him, the creative power of him, and the depths of him. We cannot put faith in anything else. He is our all in all.

When a bone is broken, the doctors have to set it. The shifting of the bones can be a painful process. But it has to get reset and realigned so it can grow back straight. As it grows the body produces calcium, which builds over that break area and strengthens it. By doing this, the bone becomes stronger and prevents that area of the bone from being weak and breaking again. It's to preserve that part of the bone. There are painful seasons in the Body of Christ. God is breaking, realigning, and replacing with greater and stronger that we may be preserved (upheld, sustained, protected) until he comes for us. There is a divine strengthening he wants to bestow upon us. When we are broken, we are raised strong. It's not God's desire for us to remain broken but to allow him to strengthen us with his power. "It is sown in dishonor, it is raised in glory; it is sown in weakness, it is raised in power" (1 Corinthians 15:43). We will need this shift, this re-positioning, and this strengthening for the battles ahead, for there will always be opposition. There is new territory for us to be released into, and we need the direction of the Holy Spirit.

When Christ surrendered his life on the cross at Calvary, the earth shook, and the veil in the temple was torn in two pieces. "And when Jesus had cried out again in a loud voice, he gave up his spirit. At that moment the curtain of the temple was torn in two from top to bottom. The earth shook and the rocks split" (Matthew 27:50–51). When Christ gave himself as an offering, heaven answered back with a sign. The strongholds of the law and of religion were torn. The earth was set free from the curse of sin for anyone who believed that Jesus was Messiah. Since that time the church has steadily put the veil back up, and religion and programs have entered in. Instead of worshipping the Lord, we worship the things of the Lord. We go about *doing* things for the Lord instead of *being* with the Lord. We've reverted back to the Martha mentality instead of the Mary mentality (Luke 10:38–42). God wants his people to be at his feet, listening, following, praising, asking, and seeking his ways. He wants those that will allow him to mold them into his likeness. He desires for us to become one with him. Everything that was promised to you was promised in the spirit that as we stand and believe it will then manifest in the natural.

The breaking that is happening is in answer to prayer. Though it may not look like what we expect, God is answering his people with favor, with grace, with deliverance! The spiritual atmosphere and the natural atmosphere must align. It is a heavenly rule for God's Word says, "so is my word that goes out from my mouth, It will not return to me empty, but will accomplish what I desire and achieve the purpose for which I sent it" (Isaiah 55:11). Jesus, the very word of God, came from the Spirit and invaded the natural and accomplished what the Father sent him to do, and his kingdom promises to us shall not return void. To align with God's Word the body of Christ must shift into position to receive that inheritance in the natural realm. Again, we received it in the spirit, but the natural must come forth. Hang in there, my dear brothers and sisters. The discomfort lasts but a little while, but the blessings of the Lord are eternal. The corrosion of law and religion has held back the powerful flow of the Holy Spirit for too long. God is breaking the power of religious spirits and every other lying spirit that would hold back his flow within his bride. God doesn't just want to be engaged to us. He wants us to marry him. That's why he refers to us as his bride not his fiancée. He's already married us in his heart. But have we married him in ours?

I don't know if you have ever planned a wedding before. It's a lot of work. The process can be grueling to get to that glorious day. Sometimes you experience the opinions of others telling you that your wedding will look better if you do it this way or that way. You can get so caught up in the details and in the opinions of others that you forget what the purpose of the ceremony was for, which was to marry the one you love and you want to spend your entire life with. As the Bride of Christ, we need to forget about the opinions of others operating in human wisdom, mannerisms and traditions so we can follow our one true love to the altar. All that matters is that you marry the one you will spend eternity with. All that matters is that your eyes are fixed on Jesus. Saints of God, we are coming down the straight and narrow aisle to meet our beloved Bridegroom where we, as the Bride of Christ will be united with Jesus for all eternity. So, take your finger out of the dam and let the water flow—the water of healing, the water that washes away your enemies. Welcome the broken bridges in your life as opportunities to travel new paths to new land with the One who paved the way for you. The One who was, who is, and who is to come—our precious Jesus is preparing his bride to become one with him for eternity. Great breakthrough is at hand. So come, Holy Spirit, come. Move in power!

"As waters break out, the Lord has broken out against my enemies before me" (2 Samuel 5:20, 1 Chronicles 14:11).

The Power of the Testimony

> Many people have written accounts about the events that took place among us. They used as their source material the reports circulating among us from the early disciples and other *eyewitnesses* of what God has done in fulfillment of his promises. Having carefully investigating all of these accounts from the beginning, I have decided to write a careful summary for you, to reassure you of the truth of all you were taught.
>
> Luke 1:1–4 (emphasis mine)

We see in the scripture above evidence of eyewitness accounts being used to document the important things that happened. The scripture goes on to say that having investigated these eyewitness accounts carefully (watchfully, warily, cautiously, thoroughly, meticulously, painstakingly, precisely, wisely), the writer found them to be important evidence in which he decided to summarize these accounts and reassure the reader of the truth that was taught. In other words after their diligent research, what they found to be truth was included in the writings to assure the people they were not just made-up stories. There was something in the testimony of these eyewitnesses that brought about an assurance of truth. There was power in their testimony.

The power of the testimony is Jesus. He is the living word of God. The Bible is the testimony of God, of his character, his nature. He is truth. "The Word became flesh and made his dwelling among us. We have seen his glory, the glory of the One and Only who came from the Father, full of grace and truth" (John 1:14). Even creation was designed to give glorious testimony to its Creator.

It's the testimony that brings in the unbelieving world. It's the testimony that gives the praise and the glory unto God when we proclaim what he has done in us, through us, and for us!

The Bible is God-breathed, God-inspired testimony. "All Scripture is God-breathed and is useful for teaching, rebuking, correcting and training in righteousness" (2 Timothy 3:16). The Bible testifies to God himself. Jesus came to the earth as the living word to testify to the Father. He testified to heaven's authority, power, and love. Jesus was the ultimate testimony.

To give testimony is to demonstrate, give evidence, confirm, or bear witness. A jury hears testimony from others. Then they weigh it to decide if it was truth. No one really knows the exact truth except those directly involved. But if the testimony is compelling, it causes people to search and reach for the truth. Jesus came to testify to the things of heaven. He came as God's very own representative. As those listening we can either disbelieve it, or we can seek it out. It is our responsibility as disciples to share the testimony of Jesus. Once we drop the seed of the word, then we can give testimony to it and how it applies to lives. This is a way that causes the Word of God to come alive for others. Instead of just a book of history and really good fables, the Bible now becomes life. Jesus came to display and be the personal demonstration of the Word.

Let's look at it another way. When we read a book, we often fall in love with the characters in the book. Their lives intrigue us and draw us in. As we read, the character develops and becomes more personal for us. We then become almost one with that character and feel what that character feels and think the way the character thinks and desire to live the life the character lived. Now let's look at the Bible in those terms except instead of it being a fictional story it's a reality and that character is Jesus. He is the ultimate love story for mankind.

Just how powerful is testimony? Scripture shows us that several times Jesus healed individuals and then informed them not to tell others. Jesus knew the power of the testimony. Do you know the power of the testimony of Jesus in you? We want so badly sometimes to be vessels in which God flows through unto others, but it comes with a testimony. God wants you to *be* the testimony as Jesus was and is the testimony. The Lord could have just taken Paul from this earth for persecuting Christians, but instead he revealed himself in such a way to Paul that it became a witness to his mercy and grace. Paul then decided to live for Christ and spend his entire life giving testimony to Jesus through his own personal experience with the Lord. How much better that God would take unbelievers and draw them to him that they would believe and receive. Now that's a testimony, to stand in front of people and say, "I once persecuted what I did not understand; but I've had a personal experience with Jesus Christ, and I'm only here by his grace and love for me to share this." A testimony has power to grab the attention of others.

The Holy Spirit is proof to what Jesus accomplished on the cross. Jesus said he would be leaving but that another would come to comfort them after his death and resurrection; the Holy Spirit came as evidence to the *power* of what was accomplished by the sacrifice of our Savior. The Holy Spirit came to live inside you and me that the testimony of Jesus would shine in us and his power would move through us that his love would draw others to desire to know him.

> The spirit of the Lord is upon me, for he has appointed me to preach the good news to the poor. He has sent me to proclaim [announce, declare, broadcast, state publicly, make known] that captives will be released, that the blind will see, that the downtrodden will be freed from their oppressors, and that the time of the Lord's favor has come.
>
> Luke 4:18

How do we proclaim? We proclaim through the testimony. I know I'm saying this word a lot here. But there is power in the testimony! You may even think to yourself,

I've never really had anything exciting or anything bad hap-pen in my life . I've lived a normal life. What could I have to offer to someone else? Well I'm here to tell you that you do have a testimony! You have been given authority to pro-claim that those captives be released, that blind will see, and that the favor of the Lord has come. You know why? It is because you have the written testimony of the Word of God. You have a book filled with chapter after chapter of testimonies to the love of God, to his grace, his com-passion, his jealousy for us, his deliverance, his protection, his provision, his justice, his power, and so on. And it's called the Holy Bible. When you received Jesus as your Savior, by faith you took into account the testimony of others or by the followers of God written in the bible, and they became your testimony. Jesus lives in you and through you now, and you are the testimony just as Paul was, as David was, as Mary was, as Moses was, as Jesus *is*. You are the demonstration to Jesus' life and death and resurrection. He is in you, and you are in him. There is no difference. He is your beginning and ending. He is your story, and you are his. Now how about that? Pretty awe-some don't you think?

We have been given a choice though. No matter what we do, we are testifying to something. Will you let it be a testimony of the one who lives inside you and has given you his power and authority over the enemy that you may live in freedom and in his grace? If you do, the power of that testimony will shine through you for others to see. You are a declaration to his goodness, his love, his compassion, his mercy, and his grace when you allow him to live through you.

Moses allowed God to live through him as a deliverer. When the plague of death came to Pharaoh and his kingdom to smite the firstborn, the Lord instructed Moses to tell the Jews to take the blood of a lamb and place it over their doorposts. He did this so that those who trusted in God would be spared from judgment. Now before Jesus came to the earth to be *the Lamb*, there was only the Old Testament. The Old Testament was the *testimony* of the saving power, the sacredness of the blood of the lamb. It testified to the power of the blood to save from death because the spirit of death passed by every home that had the lamb's blood over its doorpost. This was a foreshadow to the power of the blood of the Lamb of God, the one who was to come—Jesus.

Did you know that giving a testimony to healing or deliverance can actually cause others around you to get healed or delivered? It's happened in many Christian conferences and church services around the world, and even at people's kitchen tables! People began giving testimony to God's healing work, and others were suddenly healed. God's presence comes with the testimony. There is no greater testimony than the spirit of the living God. When you experience a touch from the living God himself, you know without a doubt that God is real.

John the Baptist's whole ministry was to give testimony to the coming Messiah. He was preparing the people for what was to come; that way they would recognize him when he came. God even says he does nothing unless he reveals it to his prophets first. God revealed Jesus through Moses, through Abraham, through John, and many more before he sent him to the earth.

> If I were to testify on my own behalf, my testimony would not be valid. But someone else is also testifying about me, and I can assure you that everything he says about me is true. In fact you sent messengers to listen to John the Baptist, and he preached the truth. But the best testimony about me in not from a man, though I have reminded you about John's testimony so you might be saved.
>
> John 5:31–45

We testify to Jesus every day, every time we give someone a kind word, a look of understanding, a helping hand, a hug, or a gentle pat on the back that says, "I'm here for you," or "I understand." When we give personal testimony, it solidifies the very Word of God. Now this doesn't mean that God's Word needs our testimony to be true. It is truth whether we embrace it or not, whether we testify to it or not. It stands firm, and it is established forever. But we are more likely to embrace this truth when we see God's word living in and through the lives of others through their experiences, their personal testimonies. However, the Scripture states in John 5:34, "but the best testimony about me is not from man, though I have reminded you about John's testimony so you might be saved." Now this implies that it is not the testimony of man that causes others to believe. It is the power of the truth itself embedded in the testimony from man. Does this make sense?

Let me explain. We speak forth a testimony to what God has done in our lives so others may *hear*. But it's the power of God in the truth we speak, embedded in that testimony that causes others to *receive*. The spirit of the living God bears witness to that testimony we are professing. He lives inside it because he himself is truth. "I am the way and the truth and the life. No one comes to the Father except through me" (John 14:6). God's spirit is the *life* inside of that personal testimony to point the way to him!

We are in a day where people are running from the religious structure of the church. People need a reason to even give the Bible a second thought. They think they have heard it all before when they grew up in the church. They expect to be condemned. We as Christians sometimes think they don't know anything. They may be deceived by Satan about the truth of the love of Jesus, but they are a very smart people. If we profess that Jesus loves them for nothing as his Word says, then why are we not testifying to this? Why are we judging them harshly? "How can you say to your brother, 'Brother, let me take the speck out of your eye,' when you yourself fail to see the plank in your own eye? You hypocrite, first take the plank out of your eye, and then you will see clearly to remove the speck from your brother's eye" (Luke 6:42).

They already know what's not working in their lives, just as we do. Often we are all just in denial of it. The only difference between the believing and the unbelieving is that as believers we have the shed blood of Jesus, the very word of God that says I love you and I saved you from death for nothing. Even as Christians we have a hard time embracing everything that is written in the Word. We can know it in our minds, but we aren't always in a place to embrace it in our hearts. We are all hurting, believers, and unbelievers alike. The difference is we have been given the hope of things to come as a believer, because Jesus said so and he cannot lie. It's a confident hope knowing that this too shall pass. We need to begin to look at our unsaved friends as future brothers and sisters in Christ. Jesus shared the truth in a way that was palatable (edible, tasty, appetizing, delicious) to the one he was speaking. When he was ministering to the lost, not the religious, he spoke in words they would either understand or would grab their attention so much it caused them to think thus creating in them a desire to want to know more. When I say palatable, I'm not talking about watering down the gospel and telling others what they want to hear or to sugarcoat a sinful lifestyle despite the truth. I'm talking about delivering truth in love, in compassion, in encouragement that the Word would draw them to want this living water. God's Word is supposed to be used to build up not tear down. I can't stand it when Christians use the Word of God against each other to argue who's right and who's wrong. There have been church splits over this. It saddens me because God's Word is for edification, to build up. God's Word isn't supposed to be used to tear down *people*. It's supposed to be used to tear down the *demonic strongholds* in the spirit realm! "For our struggle is not against flesh and blood, but against the rulers, against the authorities, against the powers of this dark world and against the spiritual forces of evil in the heavenly realms" (Ephesians 6:12).

While Apollos was in Corinth, Paul traveled through the interior provinces. Finally, he came to Ephesus, where they found several believers. "Did you receive the Holy Spirit when you believed?" he asked them. "No," they replied, "we don't know what you mean. We haven't heard that there is a Holy Spirit." "Then what baptism did you experience?" he asked. And they replied, "The baptism of John." Paul said, "John's baptism was to demonstrate a desire to turn from sin and turn to God. John himself told the people to believe in Jesus, the one John said would come later." As soon as they heard this, they were baptized in the name of the Lord Jesus. Then when Paul laid his hands on them, the Holy Spirit came on them, and they spoke in other tongues and prophesied.

Acts 19:15

I'm telling you there is power in the testimony because Jesus lives inside that testimony! Here Paul and some believers were discussing John's testimony of Jesus, the Messiah. Paul then testified to the Holy Spirit, which the believers had not heard of until Paul testified of it and power came with that testimony, so much power in fact, when he touched them, they were baptized with the Holy Spirit and began to speak in other languages. Now if that manifestation doesn't give incredible testimony to the salvation of Jesus Christ and the gift of his power given to us by way of the Holy Spirit, then I don't know what does!

God is refining us so we will begin to draw the unbelieving world in through the power of testimony, a living testimony, instead of repelling them with self-righteous attitudes and a hypocritical lifestyle. I am not made perfect because of anything I have done, and I'm not perfect because I labeled myself a Christian. I am perfect in the eyes of the Lord because he cleansed me of my sin. I am now reunited with my heavenly Father because he bought my freedom, bought my soul with his very own blood. He deemed me perfect. I didn't deem myself that. I have no right to walk around and say I'm better than anyone else. But I can live as I am; knowing that despite my shortcomings as a human being, despite my failures, my heavenly Father sees me perfect. No matter what I've done or where I've come from, he says I am his and I am perfect to him. That is all that should matter—God's opinion of me, no one else's.

Did I come to this place overnight? No. It's taken time, and I do not profess to have it all down. I too am still learning to be less judgmental, less hypocritical, and more loving and compassionate. Have I hurt people as a born-again, spirit-filled believer? Yes, I have. Do I regret it? Yes, I do. Do I desire to look at people through the eyes of Jesus? Absolutely, without a doubt! Will I still judge quickly and harshly at times? Yes, sometimes I might, unfortunately. But I have a confident faith that as I continue (persist, remain, resume) to submit myself to God's refining of my heart, my mind, and my attitudes, I will judge less and less and I will love more and more every day. We go from glory to glory.

Don't you think it gives testimony to the humility and the forgiveness of Jesus when you walk up to a person you've hurt or offended and say, "I know I've professed all this stuff, but I'm human, and I made a mistake. I am sorry I hurt you. Will you forgive me?" Can you imagine how far some people's jaws would drop to hear that from those of us professing ourselves of the Christian faith? I believe if we are more authentic and transparent with one another and wear less religious masks, we will inadvertently infect every person we come across with the love of Jesus. Again, we testify to something every day by our attitudes, our words, or our actions. To what or rather to *whom* shall we give the greatest testimony to? We make the choice.

"And this gospel of the kingdom will be preached in the whole world as a testimony to all nations, and then the end will come" (Matthew 24:14).

The Breath of God

The dictionary describes *breath* as a faint hint of something, life *(the vital force or spirit of a living person or animal)*, short pause, waft *(a fleeting or slight fragrance or movement of air)*, soft sound *(a sound or whisper that is soft and almost inaudible)*.

The breath of God brings life into any situation. Prophesy itself is the very breath of God. It is life giving (Genesis 2:7). Even when prophesy contains a rebuke, it can be life giving to the person receiving it. A rebuke is God's correction that you may turn from the very thing you are doing and get back on the path of righteousness (Proverbs 3:12). A rebuke will correct you that you would not continue down a path that might eventually lead to death or destruction.

Jesus is prophesy. Jesus came to give life, God's breath of life to the people that they may live. He is God's intervention for mankind.

When the Lord had Ezekiel speak to the dry bones, he was saying to speak life into dry, desert, barren places in which the things you have been waiting for have not come together and functioned properly (Ezekiel 37:4).

So Ezekiel prophesied to those dry bones, spoke life to the dry bones by the spirit of prophesy and they came together. But it didn't stop there because there was no life just a form or structure. So God told Ezekiel to ask for the life, invite the breath of God to enter in. When he did, the breath of God came and they became whole and complete without lack. They were filled with the very breath of God and came alive again (Ezekiel 37:7–10).

There are things we all have been waiting for, things that have seemed dead and lifeless and some formless. But God commands us to speak his word, his promises and his truth into those circumstances, those dreams, all those things that have lay there dead and barren. We are to take his word, invite his breath and then breathe upon those situations that they may come alive.

Jesus, the very breath of God, commanded Lazarus to come from the grave (John 11). He spoke the command and it breathed life into Lazarus whom was dead and he came alive. Some things happen more quickly. Others take time like the dry bones. The dry bones in our own lives have had the word of God on them and they have in fact remained bones joined together, a skeleton if you will. Some of us are in the skeleton stages of our dream, our promises being fulfilled. The prayers we've prayed have brought down the word of God on those areas and formed a skeleton or shell. But we are not to stop there. The skeleton is the foundation of what's to come. The tendons, muscles and skin all needed to be put in place to prepare for life and be fulfilled in its entirety. God doesn't desire for us to be somewhat satisfied or somewhat fulfilled. He desires wholeness, without any lack.

Like the skeleton, Jesus is the foundation. But we're not to stop there, just in the saving knowledge and acceptance of Christ. We are to press on for the prize. We are to grab hold of the inheritance of Heaven which he died to give us and we are to invite the breath of God.

So many people in the church stop at the knowledge of Christ and go no further. You then end up with a bunch of Christians not living in the victory or the abundant life Christ died to give them, never fulfilling the destinies in which God placed in their inner man. There is a constant restlessness and then we begin to fill them with the things of the world, pushing us farther off the path God intended and back down to the valley of death, despair, and hopelessness. We fail to build on the very foundation. What is a foundation if there is not structure? What is a structure if it contains no life? This is not to lighten the importance of the foundation, Jesus Christ. But Jesus called us that we may *build* on his foundation, that our structures would withstand the storms of this world. Not that they would be free of storms but that when the storms passed they would still be standing because of the foundation on which your life structure, your destiny was built (Matthew 7:24).

Let's use an example of a life saving situation. When a near drowning victim is pulled from a body of water they often receive mouth to mouth resuscitation. Now one breath doesn't always do the trick, sometimes it's only on the first few breaths that you get the lungs clear of the debris from the water. This debris prevents the life giving breath from entering the lungs. But in order to get that heart to start beating there needs to be a persistent rhythm, a consistency in the continuous breathing in their lungs. Something you continue to do over and over again until the heart begins to beat and the person comes alive. Now look at this in a spiritual sense and take a dream, a ministry or a circumstance you are going through that has been dead. As you begin to breathe life by using the word of God, you begin clearing the way from spiritual debris such as doubt and fear. But if you stop there, it remains stagnant and the heart of it does not beat. But now take and apply continuous breath upon it, God's breath upon it little by little until you get the heartbeat. Once the heart beats, the lungs begin to respond and begin to operate the way it was intended to.

Many of us give up before we get a heartbeat in our dreams, our ministries. We get tired and we begin to feel as if there is no hope for life in that area. But God told Ezekiel to *continue* to prophesy to the bones that the breath of God would enter in. Continue until something happens! We need to believe God for the impossible but we need to partner with him in obedience and in faith and operate in what he provides. He gives us the tools, his word, his faith for it. We cannot and must not give up. The enemy will do everything in his power to get you to give up and to settle or to say to yourself *"well I guess that's just not going to happen now."* Like the example of the potential drowning victim, so many of our dreams or new ministries, even our loved ones are drowning because of the pressures of the world and because the enemy had caused us to look at our circumstances from our natural eyes. If Satan can get you to look at these things through the natural, he knows you will give up. We need to continue to speak life into our circumstances until we see the breath of God come into that situation and we get a heartbeat.

When a paramedic is trying to save life, he will continue to breathe even when there is no response. He will continue to breathe on the *faith* that he will get a response that shows life is present. God is searching for that kind of faith from his church. The kind of faith that continues to speak the word of God into circumstances and press on in faith even when they do not see any response at first, or even for awhile. He desires the kind of believers that push forward in the faith that they will see the death and barrenness of something gain a heartbeat and show evidence of life. Don't give up. It's not easy, but in God's faith, in God's endurance, in God's strength you can press on. It's not in your own strength. In our own we give up easily. It's only by God's strength that we are compelled to press forward and profess like that father with the demon possessed child that said, "Lord, I believe, help me with my unbelief" (Mark 9:24). That statement will encompass your entire walk with Christ. We must capture the faith that says "I'm pressing on and believing for the impossible but when the enemy comes knocking on my door in my exhaustion, in my frustration for not seeing evidence of life in that situation that you, Lord, would step into my moments of unbelief and remind me that you are the God of hope and of life." We must push through and believe

God for the impossible. He put his breath in us that we may continue to breathe that same breath into something else. His life is in us. Use it to build upon the foundation that your destiny may be fulfilled in him.

Paul planted, Apollos watered, but God gave the increase (1 Corinthians 3:6). There are many of us that fail to take the next steps so that our spiritual seeds would be watered and they would grow. The watering is to sit under teaching, to read the life giving word of God and to spend time in his presence. The watering is also to speak life; the very word of God into those seeds you've planted that in due season God would breathe on it and cause it to sprout and create results.

Elisha told his servant Gehazi to lay his staff upon a child that had died (2 Kings 4). Gehazi did but nothing happened. But then Elisha arrived and without hesitation he prayed. Then he laid his body upon the child placing his hands upon the child's hands and placing his mouth upon the child's mouth. The child's body began to grow warm, however Elisha didn't stop there. He waited to see if there was a heartbeat, evidence of life. Then he did this again but this time the child's eyes opened because the breath of God came into the child's body once again. Peter's shadow healed so why couldn't a staff that carried a transfer of anointing bring this child back to life? And why didn't the heavily anointed prophet of God bring the child back to life the first time he lay on the child's body? I believe God wanted to illustrate that persistence is key and that there was nothing of man that could perform this miracle. God had to step on the scene. Only God can create and give life. But Elisha needed to push through despite the lack of what he saw, partner with God and believe him for the impossible. Not only that, Elisha prayed to God. I believe by praying to God he asked for the breath of God to enter in. At the second attempt Elisha persisted, God moved and his breath, his life entered that child. Elisha kept breathing into that child until God answered it with the heartbeat—the evidence of life.

Continue to speak God's word and ask for his breath, his life to enter into the dry areas that they may resurrect from the dead. Keep persisting until God intervenes and you get a heartbeat, a sign that life is present. Then continue to nurture that life. Thank God for the life, and praise him for the life he put into your situation, because without God's breath there is no life.

Jesus gave up his breath on the Cross and it expelled into the atmosphere that we may have it (Mark 16:37). One of the best ways to honor his death and resurrection it to take up the life he died to give us and let him resurrect those areas with his breath. The victory is ours. For in Christ, there is no longer death, only evidence of life!

Push Through

A few years back I was going through a time spiritually when I didn't know where I was and where I was going. I had this vision of me in a dense fog, and as I was walking through not knowing what was lying on the other side, I heard the Lord say, "Push through." The understanding was that as I continued to push through I would get to the other side and then I would see clearly. Later at a church I was attending, a minister shared a vision she saw of me walking through giant spider webs and they kept sticking to me. I kept trying to walk forward, but all the webs kept sticking to me, and I kept trying to shake them off. And in confirmation of my previous vision from the Lord, I was told through the minister to "Push through."

Sometimes when we think of pushing through, we think it means we need to do this in our own strength. But that is not what God has intended. God means to push through in faith, in trust, in obedience, and in prayer. The Bible even says to pray without ceasing (stop, come to an end, die down, die away, finish, conclude). We are commanded to continuously pray without giving up.

I heard someone tell a story one time about a man whom God told to push on this large rock. So the man pushed and he pushed, and it was heavy; and this man kept pushing until one day he realized the rock hadn't moved, not even an inch. He became very discouraged and complained to the Lord saying that it was a waste of his time and that no matter how hard he tried to push that rock, he couldn't get it to move. The Lord responded to him and said, "I told you to push on the rock, not to move it."

Only God can move the rock. God will often keep us occupied doing what he instructed us to do while he is busy making the plans and arrangement for the blessings. He's lining things up for the better blessing and preparing to set you up for something bigger than you could have either hoped or imagined for yourself... all for his glory. We just need to surrender our agenda for results from our own hands. God doesn't need us; he wants us. He wants us to partner with him. We like to make it about our efforts and our results, and then we just say God did it. But God doesn't want credit for those things that are not of him. God doesn't need our credit. He has a pretty awesome track record of his own accomplishments... all without the help of man. We need to do what God instructs us to do—*push through!*

Let's look at this story another way. God commands us to push on *the Rock*, Christ Jesus. In essence he's saying we are to lean into him until the appointed time when he will *suddenly* move. God is full of suddenlies. Some of the greatest words in Scripture are "suddenly God" or "but then God." He is the God of intervention. But he wants to know if you will continue to push through despite what it feels or looks like. Will you continue to lean into him through prayer, praise, and worship until he moves on your behalf?

Push means to drive, set in motion, urge, persuade, advocate, or get behind. Will we *drive* the Lord by our persistence and faithfulness to move? Will we *set in motion* for him a strong desire to answer our requests? Will we *urge* or *persuade* the Lord to release a "suddenly" in our lives? Will we *get behind* the Lord's agenda and follow his leading, his direction? If we push on the rock, we will be doing all of these things in one simple act of faith. Now understand we are not manipulating the Lord to our will or our timing, nor are we performing for his blessing. Instead we are being persistent and motivated to press on in the faith until something happens—until *God* happens in your circumstance! All throughout Scripture you will see how God showed up for those who were desperate for his mighty hand to move on their behalf. God can tell a difference between the Hannahs (1 Samuel 1:10–19) and those that are doing nothing and waiting for God to bless them with the winning lotto ticket. God's plan doesn't always make us comfortable, but it *will* make us disciples.

Let me share from experience, sometimes you have to knock repeatedly until that door opens or God redirects you to another door that he opened for you. "Knock and the door will be opened to you" (Luke 11:9). My husband continuously knocked on the door of a large company in between other jobs. The enemy was persistent in causing all kinds of blockades. My husband was often on the phone with many who said they never had his application on file, and they even temporarily lost his pre-consideration test scores. Time after time he ran into walls. I myself had doubts wondering if that was the door God wanted him to go through. But my husband was more persistent and kept up the emails and phone calls and applied and reapplied for many different positions within that company. He became more persistent than the enemy, and after three years of knocking on that employer's door, he landed a face-to-face interview. Within a week he was *suddenly* hired. It was the breakthrough he needed for himself and for our family. He pushed through.

Noah was a great example of someone who pushed through. He continued to build an ark while being slandered and teased for 120 years. Imagine 120 years passing by before you saw results from what God commanded you to do in faith? Moses pushed through by crossing the Red Sea in trust while an entire enemy army pursued them. At that time, they were considered to be the best army in the world and they were in hot pursuit to slaughter the Jews. But God intervened, and Pharaoh's army perished while the Jews were delivered as promised.

Joseph shared God-given dreams and visions with his brothers in faith only to have them become jealous, throw him into a hole, then sell him into slavery. Through the entire time, Joseph pushed through in his faith in God's goodness despite all the *seemingly* wrong turns his life took. And yet God had a bigger, better plan to align and reposition Joseph for greatness, all the while giving God glory.

In the book of Ezra, the people of Judah were rebuilding the temple through opposition for years as many tried to prevent them from rebuilding. They were frightened, bribed, and threatened by their enemies who worked against them to frustrate their efforts. The opposition was so great that the building actually stopped for several years—a complete standstill. The enemy thought he had his way permanently, *but then* God gave favor to them by influencing King Darius to allow the rebuilding to resume.

God granted favor! If we keep on in persistence to what he has called us to do no matter what the circumstances look like, no matter who opposes us, God grants favor to us even in the eyes of our enemies.

During a particular season in my journey with Christ, my husband and I had to humble ourselves and borrow some money from some family friends. They wanted to talk with us first, and I did not want to go. I felt ashamed. I had been praying and asking God to intervene for us financially, and he chose to do it this way. I did not want to go, and I made that very clear to God. But then the Lord spoke to me and said, "You will go because I have decided to provide for you in this particular way." I had some choices to make. I could decide not to go because of fear, guilt, shame, and pride and lose out on a blessing, or I could trust the Lord and his direction whether or not I knew what it was going to look like and sound like. I pushed through despite my feelings or my ideas of how things should work out. Well, unfortunately the enemy gave me a bit of a tongue lashing because those we borrowed from were in operation of their flesh and not their spirit unbeknownst to them. Honestly, I believe they thought they were giving me good sound advice and judgment for my betterment. Although their hearts may have been in the right place, the enemy used the opportunity and a momentary lack of spiritual discernment to rise up against me to bring confusion and shame. Though I felt as if a great army of criticism was against me, God upheld me in the safety of his arms. They were just man's opinions and words, and God made that clear when he reminded me shortly after the meeting that the words spoken were in direct conflict with scripture, his Word. Despite all of this, God gave us favor, and they lent us the money. God chose to provide for me and my family through those who didn't agree with my walk in Christ. The important thing was that I was in agreement with the Lord. I aligned with his plans and purposes and pushed through. Even more miraculous was that God provided in another way so we could have that personal loan paid off within weeks. The Lord had liberated me! He can use people that don't agree to bless you any way he desires. Though our friends didn't understand all that God was doing in my life at the time, I am thankful to them that they had decided to be obedient to God's tug on their hearts and provide for us anyway.

Nehemiah desired to rebuild the wall in Jerusalem. He prayed and fasted before the Lord for the walls to be rebuilt for the protection of Jerusalem. Much like the temple rebuilding in Judah, the enemies came and opposed the rebuilding by threatening to attack and kill the workers. Despite the fear this may have caused, Nehemiah was not persuaded to give up. So he stationed some of the workers to stand guard while the others worked. He encouraged those building: "Don't be afraid of the enemy. Remember the Lord who is great and glorious and fight for your friends, your families and your homes!" (Nehemiah 4:14). From that point on half of the people worked while the other half stood guard.

Sometimes when we are up against a wall or an army of enemies, we need to change our strategy or reposition ourselves or our ministries for the victory. If something isn't working, then we need to seek the Lord. He will reveal what needs to be dealt with or changed in order to complete the task at hand. If you hear nothing, then wait. Push through and continue on with the original plan until God speaks. Sometimes we will need to keep pushing that rock no matter how frustrating or discouraging it may feel until the rock, Christ Jesus, moves on our behalf. We must always remember that this isn't all just for us either. We are on this journey not just for our own lives but for the lives of our families and friends and that God would be greatly glorified.

Having intercessors or those who are going to bat for you spiritually while you move forward is also important. We need to be praying for one another so we may help each other complete the tasks at hand. We need unity. "Though one may be overpowered, two can defend themselves. A cord of three strands is not quickly broken." (Ecclesiastes 4:12) When we are pushing through, it's important to have others standing guard on your behalf. It is not wise to lean on your own strength. When we do we set ourselves up for failure. We cannot be victorious in the Christian walk without the strength of the Lord and the help of those who are unified in one spirit and in one accord (agreement, harmony). "The strength of a horse does not impress him, how puny in his sight is the strength of a man. Rather the Lord's delight is in those who honor him, those who put their hope in his unfailing love" (Psalm 147:10–11).

Jacob wrestled with God, and his walk was forever changed. The Word of God says that the angel of the Lord touched his hip, and it came out of the socket. Jacob walked from then after with a limp (Genesis 32:24–31). Jacob was determined to get a blessing from God. But I believe the blessing he really got was transformation into greater humility and complete dependence on God. Have you ever injured yourself and walked slowly because of it? Did you ever need help from others while on crutches? I have. It can be a humbling experience to have to rely on the help of others. But that's a good thing in God's eyes. He doesn't want us to stand in our own strength. He wants us to stand in *his* strength. And he will often use others to bring his blessings to us. It's in our weakness that he shows himself strong. You cannot fully experience that until you come into intimacy with God. Jacob came face to face with God and lived. Like Moses, you cannot get that close to God and not be transformed. Moses' hair turned white after his encounter. And just like Hannah's desperation for a child of her own, Jacob was also so desperate for a blessing from God that he wrestled all night to daybreak until the angel of the Lord blessed him. His encounter resulted in a limp and a new name. Like Jacob, we may get a few battle wounds and some spiritual scrapes. We too, may walk with a limp; but are we desperate enough for God to move the rock for us? Jacob and Hannah were desperate enough. Many others in the Bible were desperate enough. But are you?

Imagine what God can do for us when we lean on him, *the Rock*, and push through in faith. Imagine if we trust what the scriptures say about him. Look what he did for for those in the bible who followed him. Find yourself in the Word. Replace their names and add yours in there. You too are writing a great story with your walk in Christ, one of the greatest stories ever told, so press in, dear saints. Your story is waiting to be heard by others who need to be encouraged to *push through*.

Weapons of our Warfare: The Sword and the Shield

One morning back in November 2006, I was talking to the Lord. I asked him what he wanted to talk about and what he had on *his* heart for the day. He spoke to my heart very clearly and said, "Get out the armor, the necessity of it, so adults and children may know." The church needs the knowledge and understanding of the armor and its importance in our spiritual life. During my time of writing God gave me insight into the different pieces of armor, but I felt as if he was emphasizing two of the pieces above the others. Does this mean the other pieces aren't important? No. It's just what the Lord has put his spotlight on for this moment.

> For the word of God is alive and powerful. It is sharper than the sharpest two-edged sword, cutting between soul and spirit, between joint and marrow. It exposes our innermost thoughts and desires.
>
> Hebrews 4:12

For a sword use God's message that comes from
the Spirit.

Ephesians 6:10–17

The rider wore a robe that was covered with blood,
and he was known as "The Word of God." He was
followed by armies from heaven that rode on horses
and were dressed in pure white linen. From his mouth
a sharp sword went out to attack the nations.

Revelations 19:13–15

The scriptures above compare the Word of God to a sword.
One that is alive and active. The Word of God is actually
even sharper than the sharpest double-edged sword. It sep-
arates dark from light, lie from truth. It exposes the intent
of the heart revealing its deceit. Imagine words being able
to do all of that. But they are not just any words. They are
the words of God, and they are Jesus Christ, the word of
God in the flesh. "In the beginning was the Word, and the
Word was with God, and the Word was God" (John 1:1).

As the word of God in the flesh, Jesus came to divide
households, set up justices, and expose injustices. He
came to be the living example of God's word in action.
Jesus came not only to bring comfort for the hurting and
oppressed but discomfort to those who found wisdom in
themselves and in their worldly ways. Jesus is the very
sword of the Lord. He came to *be* the light of the world
and to tear down the kingdom of darkness. He "did not
come to bring peace but a sword" (Matthew 10:24).

I have since learned that there are many variations of

the weapon known as the *sword*. This discovery in my journey came when the Lord showed me a vision of a brother in the faith at a church service. In the vision he was holding a dagger in his hand, and the enemy was close to him, so close they were almost touching. They were face to face, and then I saw my brother in the faith jab the enemy quickly right in the gut with a small dagger.

As I pondered this vision, the Lord spoke to my spirit and said, "It was the quick and swift jab of the word of the Lord." It was almost like a sneak attack. The enemy never saw it coming. What I saw in this vision was very new to me. Thus began my search to study and discover the weapons of our warfare. I was incredibly enlightened as to the things I discovered in my study Bible, and then the Lord began to speak to me with the understanding as well as new revelation of the weapons of warfare.

"So Ehud made a double-edged dagger that was about a foot long, and he strapped it to his right thigh, keeping it hidden under his clothing" (Judges 3:16). The dagger can represent quick, sharp, thrusts of the Word of God, for when the enemy sneaks up, gets close, and catches you off guard. When you perceive his presence, a quick sharp thrust of the Word of the Lord is what you need.

The name of Jesus is powerful. The name of Jesus is a quick, sharp, and deadly thrust of the Word of God to the enemy. Jesus himself as we know is the Word of God in the flesh. I was able to experience this firsthand one night while having a dream or so I thought. It seemed I was in the state between asleep and awake when I walked into a house and was looking around, and as I went into this one particular room, a demonic spirit jumped on me and was holding me down. Its claws were locked into my hands with each of its fingers in between mine as I struggled with all my might to get my arms and hands free. I was pinned down. My wrists were bending to try to overcome the strength of this spirit. I tried to bind and rebuke but found I had no voice. It was if this thing had its claws around my throat as well, and I was unable to speak. However, I began to repeat the name of Jesus in my head silently over and over; then suddenly my voice broke free. I awoke to find myself still held down and struggling while I screamed out, "Jesus!" Immediately the demonic presence left me, and I was free. Talk about an unusual experience, and this was in my first year as a believer in Christ Jesus! Of course I second-guessed my experience until the following morning; when I awoke I found that my arms, wrists, and the webs of my fingers were painfully sore. Now maybe one could explain away the soreness of the wrists and arms but the webs in between my fingers? What God revealed to me about that experience was the *power* in the name of Jesus. Anything that rises against you cannot stand against the power of the name of Jesus. Even when the enemy tries to catch you off guard when you are asleep or sick or overwhelmed with other things and you are found face to face with him, you have the dagger of the Lord, the name of Jesus himself.

The real objective, however, is to keep the enemy from getting that close to you. This is where the bow and the arrow come in handy. The bow and arrow when launched can reach distances of 650 feet and possibly more. You can liken the bow and arrow to preventative prayers. These are prayers using the Word of God that are launched into the camp of the enemy before he can even assemble a strategy against you. In times of battle against the enemy, the cities would put their archers with their bows and arrows on their walls. From there they could launch an attack at the enemy to prevent them from getting near the walls of their city. Once the enemy was able to get close to their walls, it was more difficult to hold them off. If the enemy was able to breach the walls of the city, they would conquer that city. So the importance of keeping the enemy from breeching their walls was necessary for survival. The goal was to keep the enemy out of your camp and attack his camp to push him farther and farther away from your land. It's the same in our spiritual walk. We need to keep the enemy as far away from our camps as possible. We can do this by prayer. Satan went before the throne of God and petitioned to take everything away from Job. We have every right as heirs to the throne of God because of what Jesus did for us to *counter-petition* any petition Satan has set before God on our behalf. Once we understand our enemy and his tactics, we can counter-petition prior to Satan's petitioning. We can go before the Lord in our prayer time and counter petition any and every plan or strategy Satan has for our life, ministry, and our families. Ultimately it's God's will that will be done, but my belief, according to the Word of God is "you have not because you ask not" (James 4:2).

God is always ahead of the enemy's plans. When we are in fellowship and intimacy with God, when we are in prayer, he will sometimes reveal those things in which the enemy is intending to plot against you. Then you may battle on your knees with preventative prayers. The enemy never saw it coming, and you just launched a whole mess of arrows into his camp—a surprise attack. Ideally, the enemy should experience more surprise attacks on his kingdom than we should from him. God is in the business of restoring everything Satan has stolen from us, be it our health, our marriages, our ministries, or our children. We do not have to receive Satan's plans for us. We need to be prepared, and study the Word so we are ready for battle in and out of season.

"Shields flash red in the sunlight! See the scarlet uniforms of the valiant troops! Watch as their glittering chariots move into position, with a forest of spears waving above them" (Nahum 2:3). In times of battle, the *spear* was used to keep the enemy at a safe distance from the body when in close combat. It could pierce the opponent and keep you out of the immediate danger zone, preventing you from being inflicted. Even better it could also reach over the heads of their allies without injuring them while impaling the enemy on the opposing team. The spear when thrown like a javelin can hit targets that are trying to assemble against you as well. It has a similar effect as the *bow and arrow*.

We can compare the ability of the spear to prayer coverings. Prayer coverings are those that you bring before the Lord on behalf of another. When you are on the spiritual front lines battling, doesn't it strengthen your faith to know that there are others in Christ battling with you?

God is so good that he will even put your face before others you know in their prayer time specifically to pray a covering over you. I would not be able to get through a lot of my spiritual battles without the prayers of my brothers and sisters in the Lord. Just picture it for a moment. You are moving forward in the things of God and battling against the enemy's tactics; however, the enemy brings in more troops to come against you as you continue to gain ground. Now you are beginning to feel the fatigue set in because there are many more trying to come against you and you've been battling a bit. The enemy hates it when you continue to move forward for the kingdom of God despite all of his attempts to hold you back and keep you down. So the Lord alerts one or two or several brothers and sisters in the faith to pray for you. Suddenly you have them rallying behind you on the spiritual battle field reaching over you and jabbing their prayers, their spears at the enemy and at his cohorts. You begin to gain new strength and push forward knowing you have others on your side. Now the enemy is outnumbered, and you are taking control of the ground God has given you. Your faith is increased knowing you never go into battle alone. " Two are better than one … if one falls down, his friend can help him up … a cord of three strands is not quickly broken" (Ecclesiastes 4:9–12).

This brings us to the other piece of armor God is putting the spotlight on—*the shield*. The shield is often referred to as a defense piece, but it can also be used as a piece for offensive warfare. Let's look at the shield of faith. Faith isn't just what you use to stand your ground against the enemy, but it's also what you use to advance *against* the enemy. If you've ever watched movies such as *Braveheart*, *Gladiator*, *Lord of the Rings*, or any other battle scene, you'll notice that many times in battle they not only used their shields to protect their important parts that keep them alive (their heart specifically), but they used them to push back the enemy. I'll never forget the movie *Gladiator* in which all the men gathered in unity in a circle and had their shields up side by side, covering their bodies so well nothing could get through. The leader told them to continue to hold; all the while their enemies were hitting their shields. Their enemies began to get discouraged because they kept hitting their shields and were unable to cause injury. Then at the precise moment the leader unleashed the command, and they moved position and began to push the enemy back with their shields and began to strike them together. Had they not waited with their shields up in unity until the precise moment, the battle wouldn't have been as effective, and they would not have achieved victory. Now there is something to say for faith in unity. It is extremely damaging to the kingdom of hell. "Each one of you will put to flight a thousand of the enemy, for the Lord your God fights for you, just as he has promised" (Joshua 23:10).

In times of battle sometimes the enemy knocked a sword out of their hands or a spear broke. When this happened, many used their shields to not only protect themselves but also to hit back and knock their enemy off his footing so they might have a chance to regain their weaponry and go in for the kill. Shields are very important weapons of warfare. They are an offensive piece as much as a defensive piece of armor. Like your faith, not only does it serve as a defense when the enemy is striking at your heart, but it serves as an *offense* to help you push through the enemy's attacks. When you push through in faith, you continue to gain ground. Even if you are standing still holding that shield of faith, you have not lost ground against the enemy. Faith will help you to persist when you are exhausted from the battle and your arms are too tired to sling that sword. It provides you a pause or hesitation to regain your posture as your feet are firmly planted and your heels are digging in. That is the picture of faith, heels dug in so your feet are firmly planted and nothing will move you from your position. When you regain your posture or even switch direction, you can then move forward and begin slinging that sword again. The sword and the shield work together hand in hand. Think of it as a one-two combo: hit/block, or sword/shield, or speak the Word of God/stand firm and push through in faith. The two, the sword of the Word of God and the shield of faith are a powerful and deadly combination to the enemy. "Be on your guard; stand firm in the faith; be men of courage; be strong" (1 Corinthians 16:13).

Although God highlighted the sword and the shield in my study time with him, it would be remiss if I did not mention *praise*. Praise is another very important weapon of warfare although its importance is often overlooked by some. Praise causes confusion in the enemy's troops. They can't stand the praises of God's people because it ushers in the presence of God. He inhabits the praises of his people.

The enemy cannot stand being in the presence of God. It renders him completely helpless. *Praise is a sword and a shield.* Praise scatters the enemy, as a sword and it shields us in a protective cocoon of the presence of God around us. The Lord is our shield. "After this, the word of the LORD came to Abram in a vision: "Do not be afraid, Abram. I am your shield, your very great reward" (Genesis 15:1).

In order to adequately praise him, it is essential for us to know the Word of God. Without the knowledge of God's character, how can we effectively praise him the way he deserves to be praised? How can we worship him in bold faith without knowing his promises? How do you sing the praises of someone you don't know? If who he is and what he's promised you as his child hasn't penetrated your heart, then you need to study the bible and discover your Creator and what he's given you so your praises will not just be mere words. He desires for you to know him intimately. We are in a time where we as the church need to step it up. We need to grow to that place of serenading our beloved with our hearts not just words. It's the difference between Cain's offering and Abel's offering. Abel gave God his best, while Cain did not. We know from Scripture that God did not receive Cain's offering. God looks into the heart of man. Cain's heart was not in what he offered. By not giving God his best, Cain's actions implied that God didn't deserve his best. If we just give him lip service how effective can our praises be? If we just sing to sing because "that's what we are supposed to do," it's not much of an offering. How would you treat a friend who saved your life? You would be forever grateful and probably spend the rest of your life thanking that person and looking for ways to show your gratitude for what was done, correct? When we praise God with all our hearts, we are lifting up grateful gestures to the one who gave his life for us. He's the one who took our punishment and the one who continues to keep watch over us and our families day and night. He goes before us and with us into every battle, and he gives us all that we need for the battle including the victory! We don't go in ill-equipped. He's never too busy for us and always there to give us that refreshing drink of water, his spirit, in times of battle fatigue. How would you want to repay someone for that kind of dedication to you, that kind of generosity because they love you that much? Praise is our way of expressing our gratitude to the one who never tires, the one who never sleeps and always keep watch over us. He is the one who feeds our spirit when it hungers, the one who fills us to overflowing with all that we need. Praise not only releases his presence but voices the faith that lives in us— *his* faith! That kind of faith resonates into the atmosphere and intimidates our enemies.

"The kingdom of God suffers violence but the violent taketh by force" (Matthew 11:12). We need to become violent against the enemy in this end-time hour. Though we do not know the exact time and date the Lord will return, we know we are nearer to it than anyone ever was before us. It is inevitable. He is coming. There is still much ground to claim for Christ and so little time to claim it. The enemy of our souls is at work, and just as God has a battle plan for the end times, the enemy has a secret end-time battle plan too. However, it's only a secret to us. It's no secret to God. For nothing shall be hidden from God's sight. God wants to reveal the enemy's end-time battle plan. He wants to alert us and reveal to us the secrets of the enemy. He also wants to reveal to us the secrets of his own battle plan. We can only know these things when we are in his presence, when we are in intimate fellowship with him. Praise brings us there. You see intimacy with the Father is also a weapon. To know him is to know the Word of God. To know him is to elevate your faith in ways you could not imagine. To know him is to trust him in an unwavering confidence. To know him is to know that you have been given all authority over the enemy. To know him is to know that you have victory as your outcome and all of heaven is backing you. To know him in this intimate way is to know that "neither death nor life nor angels nor demons … nothing can separate you from the love of God" (Romans 8:38). That in itself, my dear brothers and sisters, is the *ultimate* weapon—to know who you are in Christ and how very much he loves you.

Prepare for war, saints! Raise your shields, swing your swords, and sing praises to your King, knowing the victory is already yours if you believe, receive, and proceed!

Agreement with Heaven

In 2007 I had a personal revelation of what it means to be in agreement with heaven. I had been reading a book by a Christian author that spoke of loss and the inability in our humanness to comprehend the *why* in it. The author went on to explain that in God's sovereignty, whatever God has allowed the enemy to steal must be repaid back unto us in sevenfold (Proverbs 6:30–31).

Instantly the Lord spoke to my heart, and revelation came flooding in. My understanding was opened in the spirit realm. Let's say, for example, if a ministry moving in the miracles, signs, and wonders of God was suddenly to shut down or a church split occurred and the ministry ended, God would repay what the enemy stole from the righteous in sevenfold. If a ministry didn't run its intended course, God would raise up seven more ministries with a similar powerful anointing in the spirit. The same would go if a highly anointed minister was suddenly stricken with illness and their life was cut short. God would raise up seven more ministers with a similar great anointing to flood the earth for the kingdom of Christ. But here's the best part of this: the Lord revealed that whatever the enemy has stolen from you is also sown as seed. God does not miss anything. He sees everything that was taken before it's time. Yes God allowed it but for greater purpose, to return unto the earth seven times the greatness of what was taken. Job was stripped of everything except his life, but when it was all said and done, Job had sown seeds of faithfulness and loyalty, by not blaspheming God. Even though he didn't understand all that was happening to him, the purpose of it, he still maintained his faith and trust in God and refused to curse the Lord even though many close to him including his own wife said he should. God returned back unto him everything the enemy stole from him and then some. God is a God of justice, and he sees what has been done to his people.

Many times in scripture God allowed his people to be punished by their enemies; however, the enemy took too much pleasure and went further than God had intended them to go. Even though God allowed the enemy to plunder his own people for their disobedience, he still sets limits. When the enemy oversteps those limits, God uses it to bless his people by punishing or often times obliterating their enemy. Because the enemy was unmerciful and God is a God of mercy, he took it as his spiritual mandate to declare justice (Jeremiah 50).

Do we experience trials and stripping from time to time, season to season? Yes we do; however, God sets the limits, and God is never unjust. Satan thoroughly enjoyed the torture and crucifixion of our Lord and Savior Jesus. Satan was merciless through men, yet God allowed it because he knew the better plan and purpose—the destruction of the reign of the kingdom of darkness over God's children and the redemption of them back into relation with the Father. Are you aware that had Satan known what would come of this he would not have done what he did to Jesus? He wouldn't have dared to spill one single drop of the life-giving, life-redeeming blood that Jesus carried in him. For one drop is all it took to tear down the kingdom of darkness and cleanse the human race of all sin. God's ways are so much higher, and God will confound those that consider themselves wiser, especially Satan.

Suffering, sacrifice, and obedience are all seeds sown in the spirit realm. Seeds are not limited to financial giving. Let's look at Hannah, for instance; she sowed seeds of not only prayer and tears but of suffering, of sincerity, and of a promise or vow she made to God if he would bless her with a child. She promised that she would give that child back unto God for his glory and his purposes. She came into agreement with heaven and said, "Lord, I desperately want a child and if you would grant me the request, the cry of my heart, I will give that child back unto you as your very own" (1 Samuel 1:11).

I assure you the thought did not come from her. The thought was already placed in her, birthed there in the spirit by God. He wanted and needed a child who would be his next obedient and mighty servant, a prophet and priest unto him. And Hannah was whom he chose. She didn't have to come into agreement with heaven, but she did. She followed through on that agreement. That child was sown as seed. Her sacrifice and obedience unto the

Lord sowed a seed. And she reaped from that seed a harvest. She received many more children from God. Had she not made good on her promise or vow, she may have only received the one child and remained barren afterward or the enemy may have even taken the one she had, and then she would have had none. But thankfully, Hannah came into agreement with heaven, and Samuel, a mighty and righteous servant of the Lord, was born for God's purposes and for his glory.

Jesus came into agreement with heaven in the garden of Gethsemane when he surrendered his own agenda and his own will and said, Lord, not my will but yours be done. He could have said, "You know, no thanks, Lord. This doesn't sound so good for me; and none of these people really deserve this anyway, so why should I suffer for those who won't even receive what I'm going to do for them?" Instead, he looked past what he saw and what he felt and trusted in his Creator, his heavenly Father because he knew the Lord had his reason which was to save the ones that *would* receive his gift of salvation. Jesus sowed himself as seed (Galatians 3:19). He laid down his own life in sacrifice, obedience, tears, and in love, all of which were seeds, despite the grief and fear he momentarily felt in that garden before his crucifixion. He came into agreement with heaven's plans and purposes, and he was strengthened to endure what was to come because he put his trust in his heavenly Father's ways.

The revelation from God that I received on a personal level compelled me to write this message. It was in 2002, the beginning of my spiritual walk with the Lord, that my very first pregnancy failed, and I lost the life of my unborn child. In some ways I was thankful that I hadn't quite made it to the second trimester yet, but in other ways it was a painful loss. No one could tell me different, but I felt the very moment that little soul left my body to be with the Lord. I barely had a chance to experience the excitement of my pregnancy, and suddenly my child was gone. Leading up to it, I had been spotting, or bleeding prematurely, and was on bed rest to prevent such a thing from happening. I had prayed that it would all be all right and asked the Lord to protect my baby. But there came a time where the bleeding got worse, and I was fearful of what would happen. In desperation I cried out to the Lord, and I said, "If you must take my child, I ask that you do it quickly because I can't do this for weeks on end." It was too torturous. God was merciful; and within a little over twenty-four hours, I felt my baby's soul slip from my body, and I knew in my heart before the doctor's appointment confirmed it that I had lost the life of my first child. My child never left my womb; the heart just stopped beating.

The Lord explained to me that before I even knew what it meant back then, I had come into agreement with heaven. In my own words I had surrendered my plans, my desires for my pregnancy, for my child and gave them to the Lord. I had sown my unborn child as seed unto the Lord. When I uttered the words of surrender unto my heavenly Father knowing there was nothing I could do in my own strength, I came into alignment with heaven's purpose and plans. Do I know exactly why my child had to go so soon? No, I don't. I could venture to guess many things, but as for an exact answer, I do not know. Only the Father knows in his ultimate wisdom. But what I do know is that God is a God of justice and he is a God of mercy and he honors his promises and receives every seed we sow unto him and he multiplies it (Psalm 126:6).

I am happy to say that I have three beautiful children, a precious girl and two adorable boys. We are blessed because God is a good God and he continues to give unto his children abundantly. It just may not look the way we think it will look. But it will look exactly the way God sees it, for his view is far superior and he carries the divine wisdom and understanding to work all things out for the good of those who love him (Romans 8:28).

God receives everything you sow unto him: time, tears, obedience, faith, trust, finances, loss, love, sacrifice, surrender, praise, etc. Every one of us has either lost something or had something stolen from us, be it a dream, a ministry, a career, our health, our finances, or someone we knew and loved. We may not have known it at the time, but we have sown seeds. God received them, and when you come into agreement with heaven for them, you will experience the multiplication of the harvest of those seeds (Mark 4:8). Nothing precious is ever completely lost or forgotten. Heaven remembers and takes note, and the enemy will regret the day he ever took anything from you. You are God's beloved, and he is your Vindicator. Do not look back on what you have lost. Press forward knowing you came into agreement with heaven's plans and sowed precious seed that will reap a bountiful harvest for not only you but for generations to come. Abraham did and became the father of many nations. Joseph did and preserved the life of his family members. Esther did and saved the lives of the Jewish nation. Mary did and birthed our Savior. John the Baptist did to point the way to the coming Messiah, and Jesus did. Jesus sacrificed and came into agreement with heaven that he would be the Redeemer of all mankind for those who believed. You can do it too because you know what the outcome is no matter what you are enduring or have endured. God promises the outcome to be victorious (Psalm 44:7). He promises if you are in agreement with his heavenly plan you shall be deemed an overcomer! Let him reveal those things in which he beckons you to come into agreement with heaven's purpose. When you do you'll sow the seeds and reap the bountiful harvest of their multiplication. Agreeing with heaven brings unity with Christ. As one with Christ, you possess the inheritance that he has set aside for you. "Furthermore, because we are united with Christ, we have received an inheritance from God, for he chose us in advance, and he makes everything work out according to his plan" (Ephesians 1:11).

Release your Sound

Every one of us is created with our own unique sound. The way we sing is different. The way we talk is different. We even speak different languages and slang and have different accents. Just as the sounds our voices make are unique, so are the things we do and the way we do them. Sometimes we focus too much on the way we talk or the lingo we use in order to accept others. For instance, some sound more religious or seem to say the right things that cause us to think they are walking with God, while we tend to overlook some that don't seem to have the right look, personality, language, the right sound, and we devalue the gifting God has placed in them (2 Timothy 3:5).

In nature, some animals are attracted by the sound they hear. Penguins in the wild look for a sound that attracts them. They may not know what it is they are looking for, but they know when they hear it that it's the sound that they can be in harmony with or union with if you will. Let's use the animated movie of *Happy Feet*, for instance, the story about a penguin who couldn't use his voice but had another attribute to offer; his tap-dancing skills. Now

I know this may seem a bit unusual to use an animated film to speak about things of the spirit. But God speaks to me in what some may see as unusual ways, and he teaches me in unorthodox ways because of how he's created me. The Lord knows how to speak to me to get me to understand and get me to respond to what he's teaching me. So bear with me on this. In the animated film they refer to the penguin sounds as their *heart sound*. A little fellow was born different than the rest. He couldn't sing in a harmony that everyone else could receive, but boy he could tap dance! There was a rhythm in him that was unmatched because it was unique; it was his gift, his sound. Yet the other penguins wouldn't accept him because it seemed, well, weird to them. It wasn't typical; it wasn't what they were used to, so they didn't like it. What made him unique was that his sound didn't come from the way he talked; it came from inside him, and he responded to that sound in him in a different way, a way for which he was born. His heart sound looked different because it didn't stay just in the heart but it caused him to *move*, to release it in his unique way. It definitely caught the attention of others, but they were so stuck on the sound being released in a specific way that they couldn't accept this little fellow for the unique gift he had for releasing his very own sound.

Much like this animated tale, we look for certain sounds within others that we harmonize with in ministry, in work, in finding the right mate, or even the right play groups. We use it to decide whom we are going to hang out with and whom we are going to avoid. Maybe we decide not to accept someone because they don't do things the way we do them or say them the way we say them. Maybe, if we are honest, they even embarrass us. Sometimes we look too hard for someone to be a certain way that we miss the very gift God has been sending for our ministries, our families, our businesses, etc. We can even be spiritually "clicky," as if in a spiritual "in-crowd" and not allow others to enter into the fold because they are different than what we like or have grown accustomed to.

But God doesn't care about all of that. He searches for those who don't conform to programs or a certain lingo. He looks for those who are willing to do the extraordinary in him, those who move according to his spirit and who are true to who they are in him. Not a religious look or group but an authenticity or realness, if you will. Many of us want to look spiritual and act spiritual because we are looking for acceptance from those in spiritual authority. Some of us carry a spiritual authority in the church, and we feel we need to hold ourselves a certain way in order to fulfill that role so others will think more highly of us. Maybe we want to impress others (Acts 25:27). There are even many of us who will deny we want to impress others. But the truth is we have all cared what others have thought about us at one time or another, even when we didn't want to. Maybe it's not just outsiders we look for acceptance from, but maybe it's family members. However, the only way to find true acceptance is through Christ, to begin to see ourselves through his eyes and accept ourselves for who he has created us to be. This little penguin grew up an outcast because of his happy feet and he had no vocal sound like the others. His father was even embarrassed and ashamed of his son's ability because of what others would think in the community. But the little penguin did find a group that would accept him, another breed of penguins who saw him as refreshingly different. They perceived his tap-dancing skills as a fresh new sound. They saw it as an extraordinary gift, and they celebrated and welcomed it because it was unique.

We see the same example with Jesus. There were those in the religious law that just couldn't believe that Messiah would come in a different way or that he would look different, speak differently, and even act differently than what they expected. They were looking for someone more like themselves, and yet Jesus, our Messiah, came clothed in humility. He did not ride down on a cloud announcing himself with a host of heavenly beings, not yet anyway, but came born as a tiny little helpless baby who needed to be cared for and fed by a mother, a human mother. God was born in humility, and when he returns it will be on a cloud and clothed in majesty for he has every right to be exalted. He alone is worthy. He is the very example of his word that says those that are last shall become first and those that are weak are made strong. He became last to become first, and he became weak to become strong. Jesus was the example for heavenly characteristics and attributes. Jesus is the ultimate character example for us to follow.

The disciples received Jesus as their Messiah because he was unique to the religious zealots; he came with a different sound. It was the way he walked, not just the way he spoke, that exemplified his authority, his power, and his love. It was what drew them to him. He walked with authority but in humbleness, gentleness. He hurt when he saw those hurting. He had compassion on those without food to eat. He moved on behalf of the sick and the blind, and he said, "Come follow me and I will show you more." He didn't walk past those who were different. Instead, he was drawn to them because their cry was a different sound. Yes, many called upon his name but only for their own gain and so others would think more highly of them because they hung out with this supposed prophet who was claiming to be Messiah. They wanted the elite status. They wanted others to take note to prop themselves up (Titus 1:16). But Jesus was drawn to a different sound, to the sound of those who truly needed and wanted a messiah.

The woman who had a blood infirmity created a different sound when she reached out to touch the hem of Jesus' garment. Yes, many were touching him, and many were speaking; but through it all, he only heard one sound, the sound of a desperate heart looking to him to save her. He heard the sound of faith.

Like some in the church today, most of the elite penguins in the film were disgusted by this new sound the little penguin made. To them it was heresy that he couldn't sing and that he made a different sound that didn't line up with their idea of what sound should be made. You see, the new sound was actually beginning to catch on to the other penguins, and they began to combine their voices with the beat of the tapping of the little penguin. When they stopped their way of doing things and listened to the tapping, their voices changed, they altered their song, and it created a beautiful harmony when joined together. Their voices were illuminated, and the beauty of it was enhanced when they joined it with the rhythm of the tapping (Philippians 2:1–4).The elders or elite group of penguins were infuriated because they saw a new generation uprising and saw it as possible threat to the penguin tribe and their customs. They saw it as an abomination to the *Great Guin* they referred to as their God. Fact of the matter was it just didn't conform to their belief system of how their Great Guin was to be worshipped or magnified. They had been doing things the same for years, and in their mind's eye it should stay the same, unchanging. But as this different, fresh sound persisted amongst the new generation of penguins, they began to reach the human breed or *aliens* as they referred to them. Their sound in unity and in harmony, despite those who would oppose them, began to reach those so-called aliens and draw them in.

The lesson here is that church meetings and services will be changing because the Holy Spirit, who brings the flow, the sound of God into the atmosphere, will be invading this generation of believers like never before. Some ministries and men and women of God will rise in the spotlight in position for this great move of God while others will literally fall apart and be no more. This will happen because some will expect God to move exactly the same all the time and they will not recognize this new and powerful move of the spirit, while others will be open to God doing church differently in this end time. They will allow the Holy Spirit to lead, to release a new sound into his believers that they may release a new sound into the earth. If we are stuck in our ways of how to talk, how to look, and how to act and we resist the changes God wants to make in us and how we do ministry, we will lose our anointing, and we will lose the effectiveness of our ministries (Revelations 2:4–5). If we allow the Holy Spirit to keep us pliable in the master's hand, and we move as the ever-so-slight wind of God leads us and unites us with him, we will get in harmony with his Spirit. We will experience an explosion of God like never before in our services and in our journey and increase in the anointing God has given us. We must not negate another believer because they look different or act differently than we do, because if we do this, we may be negating a gift, a unique sound of God that flows in and through that person. If we refuse that person, we refuse that gift. God's Word says that anything you do to the least of these you do to him (Matthew 25:40). This doesn't mean we aren't to be discerning in godly wisdom; however, we need to be sure it isn't of our flesh or motivated by our own selfish desires.

Likewise we must not be opposed to God altering our sound to line up with him, in harmony with the Holy Spirit. We cannot assume our character does not need an occasional *tweaking*. Although God will not ultimately change who he has created us to be, if we are willing, he will gently remove those things in us that are offensive to others and the Holy Spirit. But he will also enhance those desirable qualities, the fruits of the spirit already operating in and through us. "And we, who with unveiled faces all reflect the Lord's glory, are being transformed into his likeness with ever-increasing glory, which comes from the Lord, who is the Spirit" (2 Corinthians 3:18). We cannot use our personalities as an excuse to offend others. The only way it is acceptable to offend is if it's in God's truth. His truth offends those who do not want to receive the truth of the spirit. But, there is a difference of offending in God's truth and being an offensive person due to our own ideas or religious ways of thinking (Matthew 17:27). We must not confuse the two. Like Jesus, we need to draw others with acts of love and compassion and accept the blind, the lame, those in bondage so that they may experience Christ through us and be transformed, not like the religious zealots who looked down their noses and outcast or discounted those who were broken (Acts 20:24).

We need to release the sound that God has placed in us and accept the sound that God has placed in others. There are *aliens* in this world who have not been reached yet with the gospel of Christ. Once they receive the life-giving salvation of Christ, they will no longer be deemed as aliens of the kingdom of God. But they will be brothers and sisters with their own unique sounds, their own God-given heart song that will *move* them to reach even more. "The alien living with you must be treated as one of your native-born. Love him as yourself, for you were aliens in Egypt. I am the LORD your God" (Leviticus 19:34). With each generation of Elijahs, there is a generation of Elishas ready to be released in greater measure. We must not fight against, become jealous, or refuse those that have a double portion of what we may have. We must celebrate what God has given them, for it is all for one purpose and one passion—to love the lost to the kingdom of Christ.

God Doesn't Want to Change You the Way You Think He Does

When we hear the word *change*, many of us think that means something completely different, something that moves from something you know to something you don't recognize. But that's not really what *change* means. Change means to vary, revolutionize, adjust, alter, modify. We hear things like "God wants to change you," and that can be a scary thing to hear. It may cause some people to run the other direction, away from God, because it gets misinterpreted as another religious phrase that says you are no good or you are unacceptable to God.

But I want to tell you God doesn't want to change you the way you think he wants to. I personally prefer the term *transform*, which means to renovate, repair, restore. Not that the word *change* is a bad word. It's not. However, it is probably one of the words most misunderstood. You see, God doesn't want to obliterate you and start from scratch.

He works with the beautiful clay he has already created—
you! "Yet, O LORD, you are our Father. We are the clay, you
are the potter; we are all the work of your hand" (Isaiah
64:8). He wants to restore you, to repair the areas that are
broken and are not working to their full potential.

Now let me explain in detail here. God's Word says "For
you formed my inward parts; You wove me in my mother's
womb" (Psalm 139:13). *Weave* means to knit, unite, or invent.
God creates in perfection. He does not create anything
with lack. He creates with plans and purposes in mind. He
invented you for a specific destiny in him. "Everything has
already been decided. It was known long ago what each
person would be. So there's no use arguing with God about
your destiny" (Ecclesiastes 6:10). We know God's Word is
truth. He cannot lie for there is no deception found in him.
So if God's Word says that you were already planned into
existence with a destiny in mind, how can you be unacceptable to God? In fact you are so incredibly loved by God that
he gave his life on the cross for you and conquered death
that you would live in eternity with him. That's how much
he wants *you* to be his.

The Word of God says after the fall of Adam and
Eve into sin we were subject to the same curse. Everyone
born in that lineage was born under the curse of sin.
"Nevertheless, death reigned from the time of Adam to
the time of Moses, even over those who did not sin by
breaking a command, as did Adam, who was a pattern
of the one to come" (Romans 5:14). When we were born
through our mother's womb, we were born into a sinful

nature automatically. But when God fashioned us in our mother's womb, we were without lack.

Yet let's dig deeper here. When Adam and Eve's eyes were opened after sinning, they saw themselves as naked (stripped, unadorned, unprotected, bare—empty, vacant).

"Then the eyes of both of them were opened, and they realized they were naked; so they sewed fig leaves together and made coverings for themselves" (Genesis 3:7). Before their eyes were opened to the knowledge of good and evil, they did not see themselves as naked because they were not lacking any good thing. They lived in the presence of God constantly. They had no need for anything, clothed or not. There was nothing broken in them. But when they sinned by disobeying a direct command from God, they became broken. Honestly I don't believe that the fruit that they ate was of any consequence. Many say it was a banana, a pear, a fig, or an apple. I don't think it matters. I don't think there was any power in the fruit to open their minds to the knowledge of evil. The power was in the choice that they made. God told them not to do it; no matter if it was fruit or a bug or a rock, the fact remains that they disobeyed. You see they automatically sinned because they disobeyed God's command. Fruit didn't cause them to sin—although, the fruit (outgrowth, result, consequence, effect, outcome) of evil brings death. Embracing the lies of the enemy caused them to sin. The conniving and yet subtle lies of the enemy caused them to question their Creator's command. They then accepted those lies as truth, which resulted in disobedience and thus adopted a sinful nature. The serpent was able to convince them that they were lacking, that they didn't have everything they needed. He lied and told them if they ate the fruit from the tree of knowledge of good and evil that they would have everything they needed. So they disobeyed. Disobeying God was sin, and therefore their blood was tainted, their flesh sinful. Once they had a taste of sin, it was forever in their blood. Once they sinned God knew they could not stop sinning because sin became their *nature*. They did not have the power to stop sin. Originally Adam and Eve were filled with God's nature. The Word of God says there is no sin found in him. He is so holy sin cannot exist in him. By disobeying and becoming sinful, Adam and Eve were now separated from God's nature and joined with a sinful nature of Satan. But God so loved the world that he gave his only begotten son, that he reversed the curse so mankind could once again be filled with the knowledge of the glory of God, the presence of God, the nature of God instead of the knowledge (experience, skill, practice) of evil.

Adam and Eve never lost the love of God when they became sinful in nature because he created them. He still loved them. God's handiwork in creating them did not suddenly come all undone. Sin is very serious and so are the consequences, so I am not making light of sin. The penalty for sin is death. But God has never stopped loving any of us that were in sin or still practicing sinfulness. God loves those that don't even know him. Jesus gave his life on the cross for *all* mankind, those who received it and also those who haven't received it yet. The destiny of mankind was not obliterated because God had a plan to sacrifice himself—to exchange his life to conquer death that none would perish. He wanted to restore us to the nature in which he created us—*his*! He wants to restore us to our original nature and our original mindset before the fall. Now that's love. He doesn't want to change who you are; he wants to change your *perception* of who you are. He wants to restore you to the former glory of who you were created to be so you may embrace the latter glory in fullness. Sin has stripped us of God's nature. Satan uses his lies to tell us we are naked when in fact by the blood of Jesus we are not; we are cleansed of that sinful nature and are now clothed with righteousness. Now that we have the blood of Jesus atoning for us, we have been given a choice to sin or not sin. When we were in sin, we were ignorant of sin. But now that we are in Christ, we have the knowledge of sin. God removed the scales from our eyes, and we can begin to see with the same eyes we had when we were created—his eyes.

The point I am trying to make here is that because of the blood of Jesus we now have a choice to believe the lies and identify ourselves with those lies or we can grab hold of the truth, define ourselves, and live by this truth. "But if we walk in the light, as he is in the light, we have fellowship with one another, and the blood of Jesus, his Son, purifies us from all sin" (1 John 1:7). The truth is God loves you simply because he created you.

That being said, God doesn't want to change who you are any more than he wants to make a caterpillar into a beetle. The caterpillar is a unique creature. The caterpillar lives in trees and blades of grass, and it feeds on the world around it. It tries hard to blend in with the atmosphere in hopes that it won't be recognized as prey for its predators. In this state the caterpillar is very vulnerable to its surroundings. There is nothing wrong with the caterpillar itself except that it is limited. It can only crawl around, eat, and hide from others. But the uniqueness of this caterpillar is that it has the ability to transform (renovate, restore, refurbish, or renew). For weeks it goes into a cocoon where the transformation happens. When it's time, it breaks free from the container that has held it, and behold it's a beautiful butterfly. Now there is something amazing! The butterfly isn't altogether a different creature. It didn't suddenly go from a caterpillar to a beetle to a butterfly. No, it went from caterpillar to butterfly. You see a butterfly is still a caterpillar, but now it has wings and a new name defining who it was always meant to be. As a butterfly that caterpillar who was once limited is now free to fly wherever it wishes. Instead of feeding on the surroundings of what was around him, he can now be free to feed on nectar from the flowers in fields. It's much harder for a predator to take out a flying object rather than one that is grounded to its surroundings. When God created the caterpillar, he always saw it as a butterfly. God sees us how he intended us to always be—free.

Now look at yourself for a minute as this caterpillar and apply this to your life. When we define ourselves by the lies we believe, we are stuck in the atmosphere that surrounds us. We are literally grounded and limited, forced to adapt to what is around us. But when we believe and receive the salvation of Jesus and see ourselves with his truth, we begin to transform. "Do not conform any longer to the pattern of this world, but be transformed by the renewing of your mind. Then you will be able to test and approve what God's will is—his good, pleasing and perfect will" (Romans 12:2). Some of us are in that cocoon now, and God is stripping off the former things of the world, our tainted mindsets and the lies on which we fed on for most of our lives. But when we begin to accept the truths of God, we have now been given wings. No longer bound by lies, we can fly in freedom like the butterfly, the very freedom Christ died to give you. "It is for freedom that Christ has set us free" (Galatians 5:1).

You are the same person God created you to be, but because of sin you just adopted a whole wardrobe of lies and began wearing the clothing of this world for your entire life. You know the old familiar clothing that says, "It doesn't matter how you accessorize me; you are still unworthy, unacceptable, and incomplete." Adam and Eve saw that they were naked because of sin and covered themselves with the leaves of the trees. They clothed themselves with their surroundings, and now saw themselves differently than they had before the fall. But Jesus removes the worldly clothing and gives you his clothing to wear. His blood-bought, life-sacrificing, death-conquering, holy robe of righteousness that says, "I am perfect, I am holy, and I am beautiful!"

"The angel said to those who were standing before him, 'Take off his filthy clothes.' Then he said to Joshua, 'See, I have taken away your sin, and I will put rich garments on you'" (Zechariah 3:4). Satan can no longer accuse you because you are wearing truth as your clothing. It's heavenly, kingdom-minded clothing! It's still you except you are now dressed with God's truth instead of Satan's shackle of lies. Now when I say it's still you, I mean you are back to the "you" that you were originally created to be—not who you *thought* you were. Now you can see yourself as the original masterpiece God created you to be before Satan threw a pair of dark sunglasses on you and said, "wear these" so you may be deceived from your true nature in Christ. Those dark sunglasses have caused you to see yourself and others with the eyes of the enemy. But God removes the darkness and lets your eyes see with his eyes, in his light, the light of Jesus Christ. His light exposes all darkness and all deception. Adam and Eve used their worldly mindset to cover up how they saw themselves because now they had the knowledge of good and evil. They threw on leaves. Isn't it strange how we look at ourselves with shame and condemnation yet God never looked at us like that? He saw us perfect because we didn't have need for anything. Yet like Adam and Eve, we try to hide from him. We are the ones who see ourselves naked and think we have a need to cover ourselves up. Satan wants to cover up your true beauty with worldly clothing, like labels and titles, appointments, stature, etc. But you cannot go to heaven with anything that comes from the world. That's why the Word of God said not to store your treasure on earth. You can't take it with you. There is no place for worldly things in the spirit realm. Nor is there a place for a worldly mindset in the kingdom of Christ.

Until the Bride of Christ begins to see herself in God's

nature, she will never regain the understanding of her dominion over the earth as she was given in the beginning. It's not that we have actually lost our dominion over the earth and over Satan in Christ, but we have just lost *sight* of our dominion over the earth and over Satan. We see ourselves naked. My brothers and sisters, we are not naked! Satan wants you to think you are naked. If he can get you to believe that, then he can get you to believe that the church has no power and she has no dominion over him. But the truth is the bride of Christ has it whether she believes she has it or not. Satan knows this, and he will do everything he can to make sure you never discover what you have *already* been given by the salvation of Jesus Christ. "And you have been given fullness in Christ, who is the head over every power and authority" (Colossians 2:10). Satan wants you to think you are homeless, powerless, moneyless, weak, ugly, disgusting, abandoned, and forsaken, etc. And if he can get you to look at yourself that way, then he's got you bound. The truth, the real truth, is you are royalty, you are an heir, and you reign with Christ. You've been given dominion over the earth and the spiritual realm, and you are loved, truly loved by your heavenly Father. "I will give you the keys of the kingdom of heaven; whatever you bind on earth will be bound in heaven, and whatever you loose on earth will be loosed in heaven" (Matthew 16:19). Do you understand how defeated the enemy already is? He just doesn't want you to grasp that truth. If he can get you to focus on your flaws, he can get your mind off the truth of who you are in Christ. Do we make mistakes as born-again spirit-filled believers? Yes, we do. Do we get it right all the time? No we don't. But the blood of Jesus, the graciousness of his everlasting love covers every mistake, slip up, and wrong decision we will make. Satan just doesn't want you to believe that Christ's blood is that powerful. But it is! Christ's blood gave us permanent rulership. But it's up to us to take hold of it, to live by it and define ourselves by Jesus instead of what we think or what Satan thinks of us.

> They dressed him in a purple robe and made a crown of long sharp thorns and put it on his head. Then they saluted yelling "Hail! King of the Jews!" and they beat him on the head with a stick, spit on him, and dropped to their knees in mock worship. When they were finally tired of mocking him they took off the purple robe and put his own clothes on him again. Then they led him away to be crucified.
>
> Mark 15:17–20

> When the soldiers had crucified Jesus, they divided his clothes among the four of them. They also took his robe, *but it was seamless, woven in one piece from the top.* So they said "Let's not tear it but throw dice to see who gets it."
>
> John 19:23–24 (emphasis mine)

Now allow me to confirm what I've been discussing with you. If we look at the two scriptures above in the book of *Mark* and in *John*, we see that a purple robe was placed on Jesus and then taken off of him before he was crucified. Not only that, but the scripture in John states that the purple robe was seamless, woven in one piece from top to bottom. The symbolism of the purple robe is that like Jesus, we once wore a purple robe, a royal nature because we, the human race through Adam and Eve, were one with God and created in God's nature until we sinned. When sin came in through the one act of disobedience, our purple robe representing God's nature was stripped of us. The robe of righteousness we wore before the fall into sin was seamless (faultless, flawless, unspoiled) until sin came in. Jesus' death and resurrection was a story of the fall of man, the death of the sinful nature and the resurrection into the nature that was always intended for us, God's nature. The difference was a sinful person could not and would not be able to conquer death because sin is death and death cannot conquer death. If Jesus just died, then he would not have defeated death. But the act of love defeated death and brought life through the resurrection. God gave back what was offered to him—a life for everlasting life. There was God's very own life living in the blood of Jesus. Jesus simply gave back to God for the sake of mankind what already belonged to God in the first place. Do you not see that the life, death, and resurrection of Jesus is the greatest love story that ever lived, was ever told, and was ever written?

What else I find interesting in this scripture is that Jesus was stripped of the purple robe *before* they crucified him. Sin cannot wear a robe of royalty. Now hear me on this; Jesus was without sin, but he was about to take on the sin of the world for a moment in time so he could conquer it with the Father's love. While he became the sin for all of us, he wore his own clothes, but when he was resurrected he was then prepared for that robe of royalty. When we received Jesus as our Savior, our sinful nature died on that cross with him, and just like Jesus we were resurrected into the original state, original relationship God had always intended for us before the fall. "I have been crucified with Christ and I no longer live, but Christ lives in me. The life I live in the body, I live by faith in the Son of God, who loved me and gave himself for me" (Galatians 2:20).

He says we are heirs to the throne. You cannot be an heir unless you are found worthy, and because you received the death and resurrection of Jesus you are deemed worthy. You are now *one* with Christ, and all that is his is now yours as well. You reign with him! "Now if we are children, then we are heirs—heirs of God and co-heirs with Christ, if indeed we share in his sufferings in order that we may also share in his glory" (Romans 8:17).

Are you following me on this? There is so much in these scriptures that it would take many more pages, if you could even put a number to it to ever tell all the beauty of the story. Human words cannot express the love that was given for us—a love that covers a multitude of sins! (1 Peter 4:8). His love demonstrated by his willingness to wear our sin and take our punishment and our judgment, covered every sin that we would ever think of committing. That's how powerful the love of God is. God is love, and love conquered death (ruin, loss, demise, downfall, end).

When you were dead in your sins and in the uncircumcision of your sinful nature, God made you alive with Christ. He forgave us all our sins, having canceled the written code, with its regulations, that was against us and that stood opposed to us; he took it away, nailing it to the cross. And having disarmed the powers and authorities, he made a public spectacle of them, triumphing over them by the cross.

Colossians 2:13–15

According to the world, your story and my story ends with death. But God so loved the world he didn't want our story to end, so he wrote a new chapter with *his* story, one that doesn't end but lives on forever and ever in his presence, in his nature. It's called the New Testament. But it's only for those who received his chapter. When you received Jesus as your Savior, you didn't receive a happy ending but an amazing beginning! So now *beautiful butterflies* go and feed on that nectar, God's nature, and you will be telling Satan what he can do with his nature. Amen?

Part Three

Revelation for
your Spirit

Living in His Glory: The Transfiguration of the Church

While he was praying, his face changed, and his clothing became shining white.

Luke 9:29

Jesus took time to be in the presence of God's glory. Being in the presence of God changes and transforms you. You may not initially notice it, but I assure you will notice when you haven't spent time in the Father's glory. Others recognize when you have spent time in the Father's presence. They notice something different about you: your appearance, your mannerisms, your attitudes, though they can't put their finger as to why or how the change was made. They just know there is something different, something that draws them to continue to gaze at you. When we carry the Father's glory with us, we attract onlookers, those that are seemingly drawn to you because you are shining his light. The Word of the Lord says "No one lights a lamp and puts it in a place where it will be hidden, or under a bowl. Instead he puts it on its stand, so that those who come in may see the light" (Luke 11:33). We aren't to hide it but to put it out for all to see. We are little beacons of light running around this earth, in the grocery store, at the gas station, the bank, your kid's soccer game, etc. Wherever we go, we spread the presence of light and God's glory. Have you ever noticed why sometimes you'll be chatting with someone you just met and all of a sudden they begin to disclose very personal, painful things that either have happened or are currently facing in their lives? It's not just that they thought you were a trustworthy person. They are drawn to the glory, the presence that lives in and exudes out of you. Sometimes they even find themselves surprised at how much they revealed to you and how comfortable they felt with you. It's the presence of God's glory in you that draws them and gives them a comfort and peace beyond the ordinary.

One afternoon, I was at the park with my kids and a nice woman came to play with her grandchild. I said, 'hello' to her and before I knew it we were engaging in a conversation about the Lord. She began to open up revealing some her deep personal hurts and pains. Mind you she just met me, and there was nothing that showed me she was normally a very revealing person. She seemed quiet and reserved; however, that day something different happened because she was in the presence and glory of God. God came to meet a need for her. Before I knew it, I was asking her if I could lay hands on her and pray for her, and she willingly accepted. I prayed for her and then never saw her again. But she walked away knowing that God had touched her that day. She had a relief and peace about her that she left with. Mind you, she looked peaceful to me when she arrived, but looks can truly be deceiving, can't they? I didn't notice the pain she carried on her face until I saw the peace of God upon her. Then I recognized the difference. I witnessed the transfiguration. The disciples always looked at Jesus as a great teacher and believed he was Messiah, but after he was in the presence of the glory, their eyes were opened, truly opened, to see Jesus for who he really was, God in the flesh. "Peter and the others had fallen asleep. When they woke up, they saw Jesus' glory and the two men standing with him." (Luke 9:32) Then the scripture goes on to say at once they *woke up* (key sentence here—*woke* means to awaken from slumber, to rouse, to stir, to stimulate) and saw how glorious (magnificent, wonderful, splendid, celebrated) Jesus was. The disciples, I believe, recognized who he was for the first time, and their *spiritual* eyes were opened. It was the glory of God upon him and present in him as it glowed and shined outward. Yet still their natural minds couldn't truly comprehend it, and moving in the flesh they wanted to build an altar for Elijah and Moses too, whom they witnessed Jesus meet with that day in God's glory (Luke 9:33–35). But God's voice thundered and said, "No! Listen to my son, Jesus." He is the only one to be exalted. He is the only one to be worshipped. Many of us get caught up in worshipping the people whom God used instead of God himself. We have a tendency to worship the creation instead of the Creator. We are nothing without God. The Virgin Mary was nothing without God; Moses was nothing without God. David and Paul were also nothing without God. It was Mary's heart, will and obedience toward God that earned her favor in his sight. She was willing to be used by God. We are all saints unto God, and we are all called to live in his glory. God's Word refers to, "on earth as it is in heaven." Well, in heaven the angels are in his glory all the time. They illuminate the presence of God, and so do we when we spend time with him, in prayer, in praise, in worship, and simply in silence listening to his voice. As Mary was chosen by God because of her willingness to contain his glorious presence within her (Jesus), she caught the attention of many because of the presence of the Lord in her. I believe that's why over centuries there is homage that many pay to Mary. She exuded the glorious presence of God. It's okay to respect the work of God accomplished in and through a willing vessel and to celebrate the impact the Holy Spirit made through that person; however, we need to be careful to worship the giver of the glory not those that display or contain God's glory. We are empty vessels without God's glorious presence in us and through us. It's the enemy that works through the flesh (the carnal nature of man) and tries to get us to exalt ourselves and others. When we exalt ourselves or others, we are in inadvertently exalting Satan. We need to give all glory and honor due to God because he is the only one deserving of such. When we do we begin to display the fruits of the spirit rather than the fruitlessness found in the self.

"At this point everyone in the council stared at Stephen because his face became as bright as an angel's" (Acts 6:15). Stephen was on trial before the Sadducees, but the Word of God says that as they were accusing him they looked at him and suddenly his face was illuminated like the face of an angel. They stared in awe for the glory of God was upon Stephen. Stephen had been operating in the glory realm because he spent time in God's glorious presence. Transfiguration happened. Transfigure means to transform, alter, develop, change, maintain. It was evident to all who looked at him. Better yet it was evident to heaven. It was so evident in the spirit realm that it moved to the natural realm. When we move something from the spirit realm to the natural realm, Satan freaks out. One of Satan's tactics is to try to rob you before you can move something in faith from the spirit realm to the natural. When we soak (immerse, marinate) in the presence of God, we are going to the very throne and absorbing the glory. You can't spend time with God and not be impacted by it. We then take that glory back down to the natural realm with us, and it becomes evident in our life. Why do you think Stephen was stoned to death? It's because God's glory is unbearable for those who are in sin. Those who are in sin, especially our foe Satan, run from and oppose the glory because transformation happens, healing happens, truth is revealed, and deliverance takes place. The presence of light magnifies God's holiness, God's beauty, and others are drawn to it. Satan does not want that to happen. Because of Stephen's ability to remain in the presence of God's glory by spending time there and then operating in it daily, he was a threat to Satan's plans and purposes. No one can stand against the wisdom and the Spirit of God in you (Acts 6:10). Stephen was stoned, and at his death, just like Jesus he cried out, "Lord, don't charge them with this sin" (Acts 7:60). Stephen's presence in the glory of God transformed him into the likeness of Christ. We too are called to be fully man and fully God. Jesus says we will do even greater works than he. He says the kingdom of God is our inheritance. It is written that we are to become the image of Christ. The image of Christ was fully man and fully God. Are we gods? No, that's not what I'm saying, but we are to carry the presence of God with us wherever we go. The presence should be so strong that even though it lives inside a body of flesh, it will override the operation of the flesh. Just as Jesus was in the flesh but he was not of it, so should we. We are of the spirit. Therefore, wherever we go there should be evidence that heaven was there. Again, remembering 'on earth as it is in heaven.' When that happens transformation happens!

So why do we hinder this in the church? Why do we let fear run our services instead of the Holy Spirit? When we allow the Holy Spirit to take over our services, we will then begin to experience the presence of God's glory. God wants you to have it; he wants you to operate in it. But too often we allow Satan to come in with his demons and dictate what will happen via the flesh. There are Pharisee and Sadducee-like spirits operating in control, because if the glory of God gets out of the box they put it in, he just may teach them a thing or two. Pride, arrogance, and jealousy begin to take over. We are silly to think we know everything. We all desire wisdom and knowledge of the world, but we need more wisdom and knowledge of heaven from God's perspective. We have a tendency to want to control what we don't understand. So let's get into his presence so we may be taught of his spirit. When we are taught of the Spirit of God, we begin to truly understand. When we truly understand, we no longer fear and will relinquish control from man-made doctrine and the religious law to the move of the Holy Spirit. Then we will begin to see an explosion of heaven on this earth like never before. Miracles, signs, and wonders will become an everyday occurrence. The shadow of a believer will heal the sick because the glory of God will so saturate the church as it did Peter. Any item a believer touches will carry a remnant of transferred anointing upon it and affect those who come into contact with it. Demons will flee from the bodies of those in which they have housed themselves, and souls will be set free like never before. Body parts will begin to grow back, strongholds where there was never favor before will come down, and the church will receive favor on this earth with governments and judicial systems. Every worldly system will have to give favor to those that carry the glorious presence of God. Because *every* knee will bow, *every* tongue will confess that Jesus is Lord (Romans 14:11). The glory of God does that. It exposes the dark and reveals the light, the truth. And the truth shall set you free! It's already happening in some ministries and in some countries, but there are more that are about to be released onto this earth that all countries would be impacted.

"In the same way, let your light shine before men, that they may see your good deeds and praise your Father in heaven" (Matthew 5:16). Opening this up further we could say, let the glorious presence of God's light shine through you that man may see (distinguish, witness, catch sight of, understand, grasp, comprehend, realize) the good works (handiwork, design, creation, masterpiece) of heaven in you and through you! Let God's light shine in you and through you that others may be drawn to the activities of heaven—the miraculous intervention of God. How we walk, talk, and love should point the way to Christ, not through performance but through abiding in his presence continuously that we would be transformed into his likeness, his character.

"Peter and the others were very drowsy and had fallen asleep" (Matthew 9:32). This is a very poignant picture of the body of Christ over the centuries. Though many revivals did peak at certain times and many highly anointed men and women of God made an impact for Christ, the church as whole slumbered. She had become drowsy while her Prince was away preparing a place in the heavens for her. She fell asleep as she continued to wait for the return of her Prince. The Church as a unit forgot about the Holy Spirit, who was to guide her, direct her, and provide her with all she needed until her Prince returned. I attended many different denominations of churches growing up off and on as a youth and as an adult, and unfortunately though they spoke of the Father and the Son and went into great detail, little was taught about the Holy Spirit. Little emphasis on the power of the Holy Spirit was made.

We are in a new era where we need to introduce the Holy Spirit into our churches. When we invite him in, we will learn even more about the Father and the Son because the Spirit of God, the glorious presence of God found in his Holy Spirit will transform our daily walk and intimacy in Christ. When that happens the transfiguration of the church will take place, and the kingdom of God will reign upon this earth like never before in the history of mankind. It's beyond *revival* (revitalization, restoration, recovery, resuscitation); it's a *revolution* (alteration, conversion, development, reform, rotation, uprising).

God is awakening the church from her slumber mode. The Bride of Christ, a sleeping beauty, has been waiting for the kiss of heaven. But she has failed to realize that the kiss of heaven is the Holy Spirit himself, who was sent by Jesus to awaken our eyes and our senses to the things of the spirit realm. Not from the outer courts, nor from the inner courts, but from the holy of holies. This is where we find our Prince, our Bridegroom, our beloved Jesus. While we were waiting for our Prince, he was waiting for us. Let's allow the Holy Spirit to transform us as containers of God's glory, transfiguring us into the likeness of Jesus to prepare us as a Bride without spot or wrinkle for our wedding with the Lamb.

The Second Coming

Now they began asking him, "Why do the teachers of Religious law insist that Elijah must return before Messiah comes?" Jesus responded Elijah is indeed coming first to set everything in order. Why then is it written in the Scriptures that the Son of Man must suffer and be treated with utter contempt.

Elijah did come to set things in order for Messiah to walk the earth, teach, to display the power of heaven, to be persecuted, to be beaten, to be crucified, and to be resurrected from the dead that we may have redemption to the Father.

But I want to talk not about the first coming but the second coming. There is a second coming of Elijah. It is a specific prophetic mantle of anointing being released in this generation today. God is releasing this prophetic mantle to set things in order before the second coming of our beloved King, our Lord Jesus Christ.

God's word mentions that we need to look for the signs and know the season on which our Lord will return. Will we know what exact time the Lord is coming? No, but we should be aware of the season in which he will come. There are many signs that are being fulfilled in this generation to show you that the time of Jesus' return is at hand.

One sign is the prophetic mantle of Elijah that is being bestowed from heaven on God's body of believers. God is equipping his church with the ability to move in a higher level of power and authority in this end-time hour. Great favor was bestowed upon the life and ministry of Elijah, so we have entered a season of great favor upon our lives and our ministries. God is not only bestowing material favor upon his true followers but spiritual favor. There have been great increases of dreams and visions for God's people. As well there have been significant increases in discernment, wisdom, and most especially revelation! God is positioning and preparing his church for the greatest display of kingdom power in the history of mankind. The shift is coming, and some of us are beginning to feel it now as God repositions us for the fulfillment of our destiny in him. A great shaking is coming, and we are feeling the rumblings beneath our feet and the vibrations in the spiritual atmosphere.

Great opposition has increased against the body of Christ. Remember that as Elijah operated in his lifetime he also had great opposition. This great opposition was known as Jezebel. If you aren't already aware, Jezebel, who has been in the background for a little while, is arising again into the forefront throughout the church. She will stop at nothing to deceive, confuse, and instill fear into God's anointed. Her purpose was and continues to be to destroy lives and ministries that are on-fire and moving forward for the kingdom of Christ. As you will know from the biblical story of Elijah, he had many that came against him, but he used his great authority and pushed through accomplishing what God set him out to do. So great was his success that Jezebel had to come onto the scene. God is once again warning his people that the enemy is advancing against us as we are advancing for the kingdom of Christ. Jezebel has been released in full-throttle mode.

Jezebel is a very high-level principality sent to intimidate even the strongest in faith and in authority. In essence the spirit of Jezebel is many different spirits. She is very hard to recognize because she is a like a shape-shifter. She can and does take on many forms or personalities. It's because of this she can go undetected until the damage has already been done. On the flip side, we also need to be careful that we don't label everything as a spirit of Jezebel either. If we become paranoid, we can accuse others of carrying a Jezebel spirit when they are in fact just hurting individuals in the body of Christ. We certainly do not want to set off another witch-hunt era. In actuality I believe it was the spirit of Jezebel that caused the witch-hunt era during the Salem witch trials. She is very cunning at diversion and false accusation as well as hypocrisy. Interesting enough the word *salem* means peace. It's quite common that the enemy will come to the places in which God's Spirit moves to stir up dissention and then divide and tear down. This is why an increase in discernment is equally lucrative in this end-time hour. Thankfully God is way ahead of the game and is bestowing this increase upon his body of true followers. Jezebel is rearing her ugly head again seeking to devour those with the mantle of Elijah.

She will stop at nothing to accomplish her will. However, we must realize as Elijah had to realize after first being intimidated by her she has *no* power against the authority of God. We must use the sword of the Lord—the written, spoken, as well as the *living and active* Word of God to lop her head right off. Elijah took hold of the revelation of his authority given by God. He moved forward in his calling, his destiny, and Jezebel met her fate, which was death. Be on the alert! We must understand our authority given us by Christ's death and resurrection. It is imperative in order to proceed to our God-given destiny.

Scoffers of Christ are on the rise. Any reference to an Almighty God is being removed from our schools, our government, and our country as a whole. Lawlessness is also on the rise as we are being required to water-down the gospel so as not to offend those living in direct conflict with the Word of the Lord. Ministers in some areas are being accused of hate speech for standing firm on the Word of the Lord. Life itself has lost value while the wicked pursue their attempted takeover of society as a whole, all of these being examples of the utter contempt of Jesus Christ.

> Look I am sending you the prophet Elijah before the great and dreadful day of the Lord arrives. His preaching will turn the hearts of parents to their children and the hearts of children to their parents. Otherwise I will come and strike the Land with a curse.
>
> Malachi 4:5

I do not believe the Lord is talking about Elijah in the flesh here. He is referring to the spirit of Elijah, the mantle, the anointing. When someone leaves the scene, their mantle does not fall to the ground and die. It is picked up by another. Elisha picked up the mantle that Elijah left behind and then received an increase. Elisha's mantle was Elijah's mantle, but doubled. As this generation has received the mantle of Elijah/Elisha, so will our future generations; the youth specifically will receive this mantle in greater measure, thus, why the Scriptures point to the hearts of parents turning to their children and the hearts of children returning to their parents. God is restoring families, and God is restoring lives. What the enemy has tried to separate, God is bringing back together. There has been an increase in a spirit of rebellion in our youth today. The enemy is attempting to take our children so much so even to the point of aborting the next Elisha generation before they are born. Satan is fully aware the damage the Elisha anointing will do to his dark kingdom. Yes, abortion has been around for a long time, sadly. But haven't you noticed that right now we are in the biggest debate and fight for life than in previous times? New scientific studies are proving the existence of life from the moment of conception, and many that are against life are finding it more and more difficult to gather evidence for their defense. God's plan is to abolish abortion! "The Call" held in Nashville on July 7, 2007, was physical representation of the spiritual fight for the life of these coming Elishas. We must continue to fast and pray for the return of righteousness to our beloved country.

Elijah had an anointing for correction upon God's people that they would turn from their wicked ways and repent to realign with God. God is calling every one of his true followers to account and is requiring that we dig deep in intimacy that he may remove the impurities from each one of us. We are being called to get our spiritual "houses" in order (tidy, neat) that there would be no deliberate uncleanliness. This all must take place in each one of us if we are to accomplish the will of God successfully. Then there are those with the mantle of Elisha who will have a double-portion increase in the authority of Elijah as well as possess the compassion and love to draw many into the kingdom. We cannot draw others in to the kingdom if we stand in complete hypocrisy of the Word of God. We cannot represent his presence and his light if we willfully go about our own business. The clean up and repositioning must happen before the great harvest is complete, and it's coming very, very soon. Now this is not to say that those with the mantle of Elijah won't have compassion and love as their motivation. Nor does it mean that those with the Elisha mantle will not call God's people to account. The anointing again is one in the same, Elisha just being the double portion of the mantle Elijah carried. This is in reference to the time we are in as the Bride of Christ. We are in clean-up mode. God is cleaning up his bride and separating the wheat from the chaff in a deeper level. When this is accomplished, the mantle of Elisha will be released, and we shall stand exuding his light in greater measure. The darkness will thicken upon this earth, and our lanterns must burn brighter than ever before with the love of Christ. The authority upon Elisha was in even greater portion than was on Elijah. Nothing intimidated Elisha because he watched and learned from the ministry of Elijah, so an increase in faith, a God-level faith was apparent in him. We are to be the examples, the teachers of the future generation that is to come. There is coming an end-time battle like never before in which the Elishas will arise and conquer the land of their enemies and release captives from the grips of hell. All of this will be through the motivation of love, which will bring about greater signs, miracles, and wonders. It was compassion and love that moved the heart of Jesus to heal the sick and set the captives free. Love is the reason! Saints, we've seen nothing yet. The generations behind us will accomplish even greater works than we have. There are souls at stake. A great harvest is upon us. The enemy is scrambling in an attempt to fight off the coming attack of God's kingdom warriors—love warriors! As we carry the manifest presence and glory of God with us everywhere we go, the enemy cannot withstand its power.

The Scriptures teach us that Elijah was one of two prophets who did not experience a physical death. There is a future generation of believers that will not taste physical death. They will be caught up in the air with the Lord of lords and King of kings when they hear the sound of Gabriel's trumpet calling. God's judgment will then strike those who are against his plans and purposes. Does this sound too good to be true? It's not. We are so near the return of the second coming of Christ. We are so near that many signs like the ones I've mentioned are already taking place. The second coming of Elijah is here. The spirit of Elijah has come to prepare and set things in order for the second coming of Christ. It truly is the eleventh hour, Saints of God. At midnight the King returns for his bride. Therefore the Spirit of God asks, 'Are you ready'?

Prepare for War: New Life is at Stake

> Proclaim this among the nations: Prepare for War!
> Rouse the Warriors! Let all the fighting men draw
> near and attack. Beat you plowshare into swords
> and your pruning hooks into spears. Let the
> weakling say, "I am strong!" Come quickly all you
> nations from every side and assemble there. Bring
> down your warriors, O Lord.
>
> Joel 3:9–11

A call has gone forth. God is getting ready to take possession. But until that hour, the enemy has been unleashed
in greater force. We must assemble together and beat
back the advancement of the enemy's troops. While in
my study time, I felt the need to grab a pen and paper and
write the words that were coming to my spirit man from
the Lord. It is in this hour God is saying:

*Rise up, rise up, oh warriors of the Lord. For the Lord
your God is calling you to duty. Beat your plowshares*

into swords and your pruning hooks into spears and prepare for war. For I am coming, I am coming says the Lord. I come with my judgment and my wrath upon the wicked. No longer will I stand and watch my creation be defiled. No more will I tolerate injustice or oppression of the widows and the orphans. I am calling those to account. I am calling those to account. For in this day I pour out my spirit upon my people the last great wave of my power, my kingdom authority. Those who have ears let them hear. You are either for me or you are against me. Assemble my people together and prepare for war. Prepare to advance against the enemy. For it is time, it is time, it is time, and I say no more injustice, no more tolerance. Time is short, time is short, and I am coming swiftly. Prepare the way of the Lord, for I am coming swiftly. New strategies, new battle plans I release to those who seek my face. Arise, arise, and go forth in the name of the Lord. I am coming, I am coming. I am coming.

The daughter of a friend in the Lord had a dream. When it was shared with me, she asked if God happened to give me any interpretation on it. At the time I had no idea except that I felt in my spirit it was a prophetic word for the church not just for the individual. Then later on while discussing the dream again with this same friend about the changes God was doing and how we desired a completely new life, a new change in the Lord, the interpretation suddenly came to me for the dream.

Her daughter dreamt that she was at an aquarium with some family members and also many others she did not know. She said people were looking at this giant octopus and all of a sudden it slammed against the glass and broke the glass. People immediately began running all over the place and screaming. Family members were yelling at her to come with them for safety, but she noticed a little girl standing near the octopus in the confusion. She began calling out to the girl, "New Life, New Life!" The little girl's name was New Life in the dream. Since New Life wouldn't come to her when she called, she broke free from those trying to hold her back and ran through the chaos and in the midst of this great octopus grabbed the little girl and brought her to safety until her parents came.

The spirit of fear will cause you the greatest harm spiritually if you let it (1 Samuel 16:14). The octopus was a representation of the numerous fears we face in life, such as fear of man, fear of lack, fear of the enemy, fear of failure, fear of abandonment, fear of rejection, etc. The spirit of fear comes upon the minds and can torment God's people so much that it renders them useless in the kingdom. Elijah, who feared no one including the prophets of Baal, found himself up against a greater spirit, the spirit of Jezebel; and fear took over, and he ran from her. Saul's fears of God abandoning and leaving him directionless caused him to seek out a medium to conjure up the spirit of Samuel for direction. David's fear of failure caused him to disobey God and use his human wisdom to call a census instead of trusting God for the victory. Peter's fear of man caused him to deny he knew Jesus. In the story of the rich man, his fear of lack caused him to refuse to give everything up and follow Jesus thus forfeiting a new life in Christ. Fear is inevitable in this world, and it will try to come against God's people especially those who are continuing to move forward successfully in obedience. You see the enemy fears *you*! So he comes upon you with a spirit of fear to stop you from tearing down his kingdom in Christ's power and authority and from knowing your position in Jesus. But it's when we face the fear and tell it that it will not stop us that we are on to something. Fear will prevent you from grabbing hold of all that Christ died to give you! In that prophetic dream, New Life was in the midst of fear. If we want our promised new life, we need to push past fear and not just call out to it anymore, but grab hold of it.

In Greek *octo* means eight, and the number eight is symbolic for new beginnings. Your new beginnings and your new life are being held captive by fear. You have been given the power through Jesus to call it forth and grab new life, but you must push past in spite of fear. Many are not willing to face their fears and believe God's promises. They will then forfeit their new life, their new beginnings. The church spends way too much time in fear. As long as the church remains fearful of the move of the spirit, of the prophetic and of miracles, signs, and wonders, they will fall into the trap of the enemy and not gain what God has given. Like in the dream, many will run from new life and new beginnings because they fear it or they fear what they may have to come against in order to attain it. Better yet they fear it because they do not recognize it as something from God. Spiritual Warfare is mandatory. It is not an option if you want to possess your promised land.

"Behold I am doing a new thing do you not see it do

you not perceive it?" (Isaiah 43:19). When we sit in fear, we open the door for deception to come in. Deaf and dumb spirits are also in operation to prevent you from hearing and from speaking the prophetic word of God. As well there are spirits that blind the spiritual sight to the new things of God. The devil wants you to miss out. The fewer believers he has to fight, the greater he thinks his chance is. He steals, he kills, and he destroys, and he uses fear as his arsenal against God's followers. Why do you think there are so many that backslide? Because fear comes against them—a fear of discomfort and fear of having to give up total control to God. Yes, God says to be cautious and test those things to see if they are from him, but he also says that his sheep know his voice. As the bride we need to begin to operate in our gifts and *use* them for the kingdom. God has not given us a spirit of fear but of a sound mind (2 Timothy 1:7). Your new life is waiting for you. God is dispensing more opportunities like never before for his people to prosper! There are doors open that the enemy will continue to try to block or divert you from, and you need to face off the enemy and push past that fear to walk into your God-ordained destiny. It's time, saints! We need to be ahead of the enemy, and the only way we can is through intimacy with Christ. God is dispensing new battle strategies. The battle strategies are new forms and levels of worship—a worship that exists on a greater prophetic level. You thought you've heard some awesome worship, well just wait. There is a new sound being released from heaven to God's people. Only those in close relationship with Christ will be able to hear this new sound. They will perceive it and recognize it as the voice of the Lord. Do not fear it because it is new. It is only new by demonstration in this generation; it is not new to the character of Christ. There is greater understanding, wisdom, and revelation being dispensed to God's people from heaven. An increase in visitations and translations like never before. For those that are intimate with Christ, translation to heaven and visits from the Lord and his angelic beings will be increasing. We need kingdom understanding to fight the good fight of faith that is before us. We are up against greater levels of spiritual darkness, and consider that you are on the right path when the devil sends troops from hell to stop you from moving forward. But do not rejoice in that but rejoice that you have your salvation, that his power works best in your weakness, and that you are assured the victory. You go in as the winning vessel. The only loser is the devil. You can only be prevented from your God-ordained destiny by allowing fear to enter your mind and rob you of your faith. I don't speak this as a vessel of God to you today with all of my own fears conquered. We are silly to think that there will not be ample opportunity for fear to come to our mind. Fear will come, but you have a choice to stop it at the door and give the devil his eviction notice to your thought life or embrace the deception. It's a daily decision, my brothers and sisters. The enemy will always try to bring fear to your mind, but the sooner you discern it, the sooner you move through the enemy's barricade and grab hold of your new beginnings and your new life!

We are living in a time when great fear will come upon

the minds of the peoples of this earth like never before. Yet God is telling those that he calls his very own, "Do not fear." For those who are rooted deeply in intimate fellowship and friendship with Christ, there will be no reason to fear for the Lord has his hand upon them. Greater fear is coming. But as warriors in God's kingdom we can fight against it for not just ourselves but for our families, our ministries, our leaders, our cities, our nations, etc. The only fear that should remain in us is the fear of the Lord himself—a *reverential* fear. Our new life will be in the midst of fear. When the fear comes upon a people know this day that it is your opportunity to run in and grab hold of what God has promised you. There is a window of opportunity, and it's not going to remain open forever. You will discern the timing, and when God says "Go!" you need to go without hesitation. In the midst of chaos and fear, is where you will find your new life hidden. Only you will recognize it. Only you will perceive it because it was created just for you. Every one of us is waiting for greater things. But our greater things are hidden in the fear. You know the old saying that one man's trash is another man's treasure? Your treasure may look like trash to non-believers and the religious minded at first, but you will carry the discernment to recognize the diamond in the rough. You will know when you see your treasure. Your treasure is hidden in the midst of fear (Isaiah 45:3). Where others will simply run from it, you will know it, and you will jump in and grab hold of it. So many in the Old Testament battled against unthinkable odds and won! They did not go alone for the Lord their God went before them with legions of his warring angels.

Approximately five years ago, I was lying in my bed about to fall asleep when a vision came into my mind. I saw many large angels with silver armor, such bright, shining silver that it was almost a light metallic blue in appearance. As some were coming in to re-sharpen their swords, others were going out. Some were molding their swords in the fire and hammering them out on anvils, while others were using grinding mills to sharpen them. I perceived that this was not just any battle but that it was a big battle they were preparing for. Heaven knows the season we are in. Do you? If not, seek the Lord's face, and he shall direct you to what is at hand.

Arise, saints, arise! If you do not take your Christ-given authority over the devil, the devil will take authority over you. There is no room for passivity in the kingdom of God. It is written, "The Kingdom of Heaven suffers violence and the violent taketh by force" (Matthew 11:12). It is time for violence against the enemy, not screaming and shouting theatrics for show, but a violent (aggressive, fierce, strong) faith, a faith so violent that we release God's new sound into the earth's atmosphere of violent praise, violent worship, violent passion declaring the Word of the Lord! Let your faith in Christ's shed blood alone be your battle armor. Let your godly confidence in who he is be your victory. It's time to advance. This is not a call to alarm us or to scare us. This is a call from the most high God to rouse us from our spiritual recliners and advance. The Great Church Awakening is upon us!

In the Disney movie *The Sword in the Stone*, remember it was not those considered of great valor or accomplishments who were able to remove the sword from the stone. The one worthy to remove and hold the sword was the young boy, who in a child-like faith stepped forward in humility, in his own weakness and pulled the sword from the stone. God is not looking for soldiers that think of themselves more highly than they ought. He is looking for those with a child-like faith who will hear his call and move forward well aware that they must put their faith and trust in the Lord. "I tell you the truth, unless you turn from your sins and become like little children, you will never get into the Kingdom of Heaven" (Matthew 18:3). God is looking for those who know that as they step forward in obedience and in faith that the battle belongs to him. For our swords, our spiritual weapons must be pulled from *the* Rock himself, the Chief Cornerstone, Jesus. Push past the fear and grab hold of your new beginnings because *new life* is at stake!

God's Pressure Cooker

Have you been feeling under immense pressure lately, as if everything is pressing against you from all sides and you are about ready to crack or burst? Although I know it isn't that comforting to hear, you are like many in the body of Christ. We are in God's pressure cooker. Now before you say, "What?" let me explain this revelatory understanding from our heavenly Father.

I don't know if you are familiar with how a pressure cooker works, but it is a form of accelerated cooking. According to Wikipedia when meat is cooked in one of these, it takes approximately 70 percent less time to complete it to its desired *doneness* or *perfection*. In this method of cooking, the internal pressure of its atmosphere causes the liquids to create steam. The steam that is normally released in other cooking methods is actually used in a pressure cooker to bathe the meat in moisture resulting in a juicy and tender meat. Where other types of cooking can cause dryness or lack of flavor and the loss of vital nutrients, the pressure cooker encourages the meat to be basted in its own steam resulting in flavorful, nutrient-rich results. Even better, less energy is expended when in a pressure cooker because of the acceleration of the cooking time and the usage of the steam to cook it.

So what does this have to do with the body of Christ you might ask? Well, we are in acceleration mode. It may not feel like things are moving faster in your life or that the results you've been waiting for are as close as you'd like. But the intense pressure you feel, the feelings of discontentment and frustration are because the steam is building up. It's building up because you are about to be completed to enter your new season of prosperity. In this pressure mode we are fully dependant on God for the release. We cannot move one way or the other, and essentially we feel stuck. But it's for a great purpose. This inability to move causes us to have to rest (lay, relax, remain) in God's promises, his faithfulness, and his truth. This can be hard to do especially when we are feeling ready to jet out of the starting gate like racehorses. But the anticipation alone causes even those thoroughbreds to shoot out of the gates without hesitation the minute they hear the sound of the bell. We are being built up and prepared to be quick and responsive to God's voice when he says, "Go!"

God is accelerating just as we have prayed. But it just doesn't look or feel like we thought. The more pressure, the faster the results. The more pressure, the more steam is built up. A locomotive requires a lot of heat and pressure to create that steam. That steam provides the power to climb steep mountainous terrain and also to pick up speed. Saints of the Most High God, you are on your way up and out of the valley heading toward your mountaintop. The steam pressure is necessary to get you up that steep incline. You are powered by heaven to reach your mountaintop. And when you are released, nothing will be able to stop you including hell itself.

In God's pressure cooker, we are being prepared to be tender and full of juice. As the Bride of Christ, we cannot continue to bring dryness into the world. "Our lives are a Christ-like fragrance rising up to God. But this fragrance is perceived differently by those who are being saved and by those who are perishing" (2 Corinthians 2:15). We are to be succulent (delicious) vessels of honor that represent our King of kings and Lord of lords.

In the past the church had lost her flavor, her appeal to the lost. But God is restoring and refashioning her with a heart of compassion that oozes God's grace that the lost would be drawn in. She will release a fragrance calling them home to dine with the bridegroom at his banquet table. We, my brothers and sisters in Christ, are part of the main course serving those that are hungry. We have said *yes* to God to be used as bait for an unbelieving world. Will we allow this pressure cooking to continue without falling away from our Creator? That is up to us. We can endure because God has equipped us all with a safety valve—in the pressure cooker it allows some steam to escape to prevent build up that will cause it to explode. Even God sets limits on how much he will allow us to endure because Jesus endured all the hardship. But trust that he has our best interests at heart. No matter how much pressure or how much steam builds up, God will allow some "venting" from time to time to release the intensity of any frustration and discontentment. Let us vent to him in our prayers and in our worship and lift one another up until this spiritual alignment is completed. Rest assured that he is accelerating in your life and that when the lid is removed you will release an inviting aroma that creates a desire in the spiritually hungry to partake of the kingdom. Press on for he will not allow you to burn. That fate is reserved for Satan.

"As pressure and stress bear down on me, I find joy in your commands [instructions, information, guidelines]" (Psalm 119:143).

The Gold

While going about my day, my thoughts on the things of God, I received a vision. I saw the Lord placing gold armor upon the bride of Christ. There is a dispensation of Gold straight from the throne of God. I saw the river of God that comes from the throne turn to liquid gold. It poured from heaven down to the earth. I then saw the Lord equipping the bride with golden swords and golden bow and arrows. This is God's response to his people who have praised, worshipped, fasted, and interceded and cried out to him day and night. The Lord has heard from his throne and has issued a decree (ruling, command) in the heavens to bless the bride of Christ. It is in response to our beloved Jesus, who has stood in the gap for us declaring us righteous before God. While pondering these visions on my evening walk, I asked God, *What exactly does the gold represent other than your glory, Lord?* He spoke to me and said, *The refinement of my bride.*

The Lord is refining (purify, polish, perfect, enhance, sharpen, upgrade) his bride. We are in the refinement process. The season of *gold* is upon us. As God's glory is dispensed in greater measure, we need to be able to carry that glory and illuminate it into the earth's atmosphere. It's similar to when God must provide new wineskins in order for us to contain the new wine he is giving. "Neither do men pour new wine into old wineskins. If they do, the skins will burst, the wine will run out and the wineskins will be ruined. No, they pour new wine into new wineskins, and both are preserved" (Matthew 9:17). Our old armor and our old weapons just won't do in this great end-time harvest. As God is bestowing greater anointing he needs to equip us to be able to contain all that he is giving us; that way the glory and his people will be preserved (to keep something protected from anything that would cause its current quality or condition to change or deteriorate or fall out of use). The old is passing away, and the *new* begins!

The wedding celebration in the book of John was a great example of this. When Jesus performed the miracle of turning the water into wine, the master of the banquet said, "You have saved the best till now" (John 2:9–11). God is saving the best for last! This end-time harvest is going to be incredible. In the vision wherever the body of Christ went they left gold dust as representation of God's imprint, his favor, and his grace. God has saved the best for last. Greater miracles, greater signs, greater wonders, greater angelic activity, greater praise, greater worship, greater intercession. This gold from heaven will explode us into prophetic intercession like never before. It's the glory, the greater glory! We are not only being refined, but we are being given honor from our heavenly Father. We are receiving promotion. He is giving greater favor and grace in this hour to his remnant that we may be able to truly run and not grow weary, walk and not grow faint. "But those who hope in the LORD will renew their strength. They will soar on wings like eagles; they will run and not grow weary, they will walk and not be faint" (Isaiah 40:31). Heaven has responded to our travailing, and God is answering back with his *gold!*

New battles are ahead; God will not send us out ill-equipped. He has given us his very best. We shall conquer the enemy as we live and walk in the glory realm. Wherever we go bringing his presence with us, transformation will take place, and lives will be touched by the glory of Almighty God. The color of the wheat representing the harvest of souls is even gold! God is aligning us and dressing us for success, for victory! We are being dressed to carry the most prized possession—*him!* It's the weighty presence of God that we are carrying.

As the vision continued, I saw a large vault with gold bars inside. I then saw the bars being delivered by angels to the doorsteps of the righteous. The great transfer of wealth is upon us saints. The scales of justice are being tipped in our favor. "Listen to me, my people; hear me, my nation: The law will go out from me; my justice will become a light to the nations" (Isaiah 51:4). Take note the scales themselves are gold—God is justice! He shall take from the wicked and give to the righteous, and it's all for his glory that our light (his light in us) may shine before men. He wants others to hunger for what he is giving us! He desires for the wicked to turn from their ways and become his very own. "'Do I take any pleasure in the death of the wicked?' declares the Sovereign LORD. Rather, am I not pleased when they turn from their ways and live?" (Ezekiel 18:23).

In heaven there is an abundance of gold. The Ark of the Covenant was covered and inlaid with gold to symbolize the holiness and sacredness of God's presence. Solomon built a temple overlaid with gold. It was a representation of God's heavenly temple. There are golden censors, a golden lamp stand, golden seals, gold crowns, etc. God loves the gold. God *is* the gold! We are being clothed with God himself! There are even the streets of gold in heaven. We, as the Bride of Christ are walking on streets of gold as Heaven truly is coming to earth. The gold of heaven is touching down. "Praise be to his glorious name forever, may the whole earth be filled with his glory" (Psalm 72:19). We need to be proclaiming "Your kingdom come, your will be done, on earth as it is in heaven" (Matthew 6:10).

In the Olympic Games the gold medal is superior. It stands for triumph, victory, and the best of the best. It is given to those who overcome, who are diligent and accomplish greatness. You may not have known it, but your faithfulness, your diligence, your pressing in and pushing through against all the that the enemy would throw at you has made you a contender for the gold. You've been contending for the gold! Lift your arms to heaven and shout, "I want the gold, Lord! I want your very best! I want to be a carrier for your great glory!" He is looking for those who want more of him. He wants to give it to you. Do you want more? While God's presence hovered over the mountain as a cloud, Moses *entered* the cloud as he went up the mountain (Exodus 24:18). We need to enter in the glory cloud, enter in his glorious presence. It's there; we just need to step into it and remain there. It is there that a refinement shall take place, for God desires a bride without spot or wrinkle. God is looking for those who will not shrink back. If you want the gold, you've got to be bold. Bold is coming with the gold. This end-time army of saints shall shake the very foundation of hell itself. The glory, the presence of God, is your ultimate weapon against the enemy. The blinding light from the gold armor as the Son shines upon you shall blind your enemies! The Lord's glory is so great that when Moses returned to the people from being in God's presence he brought the glory back to camp with him. Just the residue and reflection of the glory remained, and he had to shield his face because it was so great, so powerful that the eyes of the people could not look upon it (2 Corinthians 3:7).

As the vision continued to unfold, I saw golden eagles soaring above the kingdom warriors dressed in gold armor. There were golden eagles being released, solid gold eagles into the atmosphere. According to the *Prophet's Dictionary* by Paula Price, eagles represent victory and spiritual omniscience (all-encompassing knowledge). They are associated with spiritual quickening and earthly renewal, restoration, and transformation. Spiritually, eagles are also considered to be attentive to the voice of God. In this great refining, God is increasing our hearing. He is placing within us a quickening to respond to his voice. He is bestowing a greater "knowing" inside our spirit man. The fine tuning is at a high frequency—so high you must be in his presence to hear it and to act upon it. Be tuned into God's high frequency and listening above the confusion static that the enemy is transmitting. God's principles shall be restored unto the earth as we continue to stand for righteousness and pursue his justice. A renewal in the body of Christ is taking place. The earth itself is crying out for God to restore her, to bring her back into alignment with all of his goodness. The trees and the rocks of the earth know their Creator and sing his praises. All of humanity needs to as well! "Let the heavens be glad, and let the earth rejoice; And let them say among the nations, 'The LORD reigns'" (1 Chronicles 16:31).

I saw unity in the spirit. Thousands upon thousands upon thousands of gold-armored warriors were standing together shoulder to shoulder, and I could hear their footsteps as they marched toward the battleground. Imagine the blinding light we as believers will emit into the atmosphere of the heavens and the earth when we all stand together in unity in our golden armor, God's glory. We must join with one another in one spirit and in one accord for "a kingdom divided against itself cannot stand" (Mark 3:24). We should be crying out together for souls, souls, souls. Exist (live, be present) in his glory. Be carriers of his presence for you have been contending for the gold and the gold is being released.

Breakthrough,
Breakthrough,
Breakthrough

What your spirit has been in anticipation of is being released! I received a vision in which I saw the body of Christ like kids on Christmas morning opening their gifts. I saw a large red box with beautiful green and gold decorations on it and a big gold bow. We were sitting in front of the tree, and we were in the process of opening a giant gift box. I heard in the spirit "surprise!" I could not see what was in the gift box because I believe the gift inside was different for everyone. But I observed myself with a huge smile on my face and a light like a warm glow coming out of the box. My eyes were like that of a child—huge and filled with wonderment. Is that even a word? It must be in heaven because that was the only way I can describe what I was watching. It was complete wonderment; amazement. I was awe-filled and speechless. In the vision as I sat dressed in my pajamas and slippers, the interpretation was given to me by the Holy Spirit that we, as the body of Christ were in a place of rest in Jesus. This was not just a vision or word for me for but for the faithful in the body of Christ. Blessings were being released, not just those in the spiritual, but those in the natural as well. God was releasing those things in which you have longed for, labored for, and have been in anticipation for. These were the things in which you have stood in faith against all odds to believe God for.

Well done, good and faithful servants, those who have stood unwavering, those who would not be swayed by the things the world and what man has offered, shall be brought into a realm of favor as never before—great favor! Favor with God, favor with man, favor with the world. Many will jump at the opportunity to bless you and not fully understand why. But I know why, because I am turning the tide and you shall experience the changing of the wealth from the hands of the wicked into the hands of my people, my bride. Those areas in which you have experienced lack, you shall experience abundance and plenty, so much so that it will pour from your hands into another's and further my kingdom. It is time now for the bride to arise into her rightful position as the heir to the throne in which she was ransomed for. The bride will now begin to see herself as she was always meant to be, the way I have always seen her. She shall claim her dominion over the earth, and she shall know that she has heavenly authority in her. For the blood of my Son Jesus runs through her very veins and she shall move in the confidence of who she is in Christ. I shall arise in the Christmas season as never before, and those who would try to remove my name will not succeed for what the enemy would try to do in this hour shall only succeed in setting up my kingdom for glory—more glory, more glory, more glory. Christmas will be glorious, and my people will sing as never before. Oh the sound it will make and the strongholds it will shake, says the Lord. So sing, sing, sing! Worship me, worship me for you will know that I am who I say I am and my name will be exalted amongst my people. Even in the media, I shall be exalted, for I alone am God and worthy to be praised. Praise me, praise me, and see if I will not respond to your circumstance in a miraculous way. For I am the God of many surprises! Santa Claus has nothing on me, says the Lord. For I am the great giver of gifts, says the Lord, and what I give shall not be matched by any human or any idol says the Lord. Celebrate for what the Lord your God is about to release to you in the Christmas season and know this day that it is just the beginning of what I am about to deliver! For surely it shall be a New Year celebration!

A song came flooding into my mind as I wrote this word: "Arise, shine! For thy light has come! Arise, shine for thy light is come. For the glory of the Lord has risen, the glory of the Lord has come, the glory of the Lord has risen upon thee!"

Saints, a great move of God is being released. I see almost like gold glitter coming down from the heavens like snow. Instead of snow flakes, it's gold flakes. Stick your tongue out and catch them. Ingest it, let it become a part of you that the gold, the glory would shine through you. It's symbolic faith!

In the spirit, I heard the Lord say, *"Tell my faithful ones that they have struggled, but what looked like a struggle to them, from my point of view they passed with flying colors. But a new season, one of ease is upon them. All the laboring was for those generations behind you, so you shall receive that which you have not labored for but what those ahead of you have labored for."*

The warfare has been great, but as we give thanks during Thanksgiving, we will usher in the glory of the Christmas season and the new life of the New Year ahead! Keep singing, keep praising and thanking God. I can feel the excitement in my spirit! Can you? If not, catch a glimpse. Get it into your spirit man. Taste a golden snow flake from heaven in faith! Because your spirit will celebrate our loving and wonderful God! 'Tis the season to be jolly (cheerful, fun, jovial, bright)!

Resurrection is Coming to that which was Perceived Dead

I have a message to give you from your Lord. *Be not dismayed. For those dreams, those promises, those destinies which were perceived as dead, which had entered the grave, are not dead but merely sleeping until the right season. The grave cannot hold what I give, says the Lord. Just as it could not hold my glory, my son, Jesus, it must give it back. The grave is not powerful enough to hold onto my good. Everything you have been waiting for and seemed as if all hope was lost was offered to me. Do you know that when the seed dies, it is then that it multiplies?(John 12:24) As a seed enters the ground if it does not die, it cannot produce the harvest. Death is an important process to life. When it died it was received as an offering that it might produce abundance. For when my son gave his life for you, he deposited himself as seed sown, and the grave was conquered and could not keep him. When an offering is made, there must be a return. For those who are weary in heart, do not be dis-*

mayed, for a resurrection of all that you have thought was dead and buried was merely lying dormant, was merely multiplying in the ground that you would have a harvest this season. That your blessing would come forth, your hope would be renewed and your dreams resurrected for such a time as this. Hold on, hold on, for you gave an offering unto me of these precious things in your heart, and now they shall spring forth to produce a harvest in your life in the spiritual and in the physical.

The season of recompense is upon us. This sentence came to my mind, and if I'm honest I had no idea what *recompense* meant. I typed the sentence in obedience, and then I had to look it up in a thesaurus. *Recompense* means reward, reimbursement, compensation, payment, return. Hallelujah! "The LORD has made proclamation to the ends of the earth: Say to the Daughter of Zion, 'See, your Savior comes! See, his reward is with him, and his recompense accompanies him'" (Isaiah 62:11). The return on our investments, our seeds sown are coming forth. This is the beginning of that season! Get ready, and hold on, for the multiplication that has been prophesied by God's prophets is ready to hit the body of Christ in power, in miraculous power. It is a great wave that is coming. There shall be rejoicing. Everything you have sown in tears shall reap a harvest of joy. The Lord's people shall dance as David danced. We shall rejoice in the streets, and we shall give testimony after testimony after testimony to the Almighty God who is our Vindicator, our Provider, and our very great reward. Get ready to kick up your heels, clap your hands, and shout for joy, for I hear the sound of celebration. I see women and children dancing. I see men shouting praise unto the Father and weeping in a joyful release. Many who have watched the decrease in your life will now witness the increase, the multiplication, and acceleration in your life. They will say to themselves, "Who is this God that they profess? Who is this Jesus that they serve?" You shall be an example unto them of deliverance, healing, and everlasting joy. Be prepared, for many will come to you and ask to know this God that you profess as Lord. Be ready, for he is glorified. "Our mouths were filled with laughter, our tongues with songs of joy. Then it was said among the nations, 'The LORD has done great things for them'" (Psalm 126:2).

Those who have been your biggest adversaries shall humble themselves and desire to know God Almighty. The Lord shows me a geyser coming forth from the ground, a dry and parched ground. I hear the rumbling in the earth, and then the geyser comes forth with power, with great force as if it's been waiting for this appointed time to break forth and break open the ground. We look like spectators at first as it bursts forth; but then we dance in it, and the water rains down on us and refreshes us. There is joy, there is laughing, and there is dancing for the children of God. Your Father is blessing you. Get this deep into your spirit: your heavenly Father is delivering you and blesses you because you have laid down those precious things as offering and he is resurrecting it! It's all for his glory. It is the joy of the Lord that is your strength, and this joy will bubble over and burst forth with such power that a shaking is going to occur. The earth will respond to this joy exuding in the atmosphere from God's people.

This joy is going to be contagious. It's going to be the heavenly infectious disease—a contagious joy that bubbles over from one to another. People in close proximity will get a few drops and sprinkles of joy from God's people around them, and they will draw in and then join in! The trees of the field shall clap their hands. The rocks shall cry out, and the streams shall sing melodies. Call me crazy, but this is what the Lord is showing me. Recompense, recompense, recompense is here. Three times the Lord wanted that word typed. It is established. Receive this word, for with it comes kingdom power and authority. As the bride of Christ, you shall laugh with the joy of the Lord at your enemies. Those that come to oppose you will actually cause you to smile and then giggle. It is the joy of the Lord that tears down strongholds and opens doors of new opportunity.

I am reminder of the Disney/Pixar animated film *Monsters, Inc.* in which they used the screams of children to gain their power. It brought electricity into their city until they discovered the laughter of one small child. The laughter of that one small child was so powerful the electrical surge far surpassed the screams of many children. It may seem like a strange example, but the point I'm trying to make is that the *laughter* of one with the joy of the Lord is more powerful than the *work* of many. The little girl in the movie laughed at the monsters that were supposed to scare her. God himself will be laughing through you at his enemies. "The One enthroned in heaven laughs; the Lord scoffs at them" (Psalm 2:4). His enemies are our enemies, and our joy is his joy. We, as his bride are one with him. It's his heavenly, confident laugh living through us that will scatter our enemies, and we shall enter into our promised land.

"She is clothed with strength and dignity; she can laugh at the days to come" (Proverbs 31:25). This is a laugh that knows you already have the victory. It's a laugh of confidence in who your Father is. It's a laugh that reminds the enemy that you, the bride of Christ, are heir to his throne! Your enemies once laughed at you and what seemed like failures, at your oppression; but the Lord will have the last laugh, and because you are his, you too shall laugh last at the enemy of your soul. So laugh, laugh, laugh! You have been given permission from your Daddy in heaven to laugh. All of heaven is laughing with you. The enemy is confused by the laughter, the Fatherly joy exuding from his children. The resurrection of those things in your heart that the grave tried to contain is here. Get ready to dance, to shout, to sing, and to laugh with the joy of the Lord. Your laughter, your joy will become a great testimony to an unbelieving world. "Blessed are you who hunger now, for you will be satisfied. Blessed are you who weep now, for you will laugh" (Luke 6:21).

The Stone Has Been Rolled Away

While in prayer with a mentor in the Lord about a particular situation in my life, I heard the Lord say to my heart, "I am rolling away the stone." Immediately my spirit man understood, and I began to weep for the amazing revelation that was coming from just this one sentence. Sure, I knew what that meant for Jesus, but I had never applied it to myself. With God's revelation I knew he was bringing me from the cave where I have been held for a season into a new life—a resurrection life! As I continued to ponder this statement over the following weeks, I realized that although God opened the tomb, Jesus had to respond and walk out of the tomb in order to enter into his resurrection. If Jesus had remained in the tomb, no one else would have the opportunity to experience or witness the power of the miracle. More importantly neither would *he*.

The Lord is offering an opportunity to all of us. He has removed the heavy stone and created an opening, a *kairos* moment for you. *Kairos*, a Greek word, is described in

Wikipedia as "a passing instant when an opening appears which must be driven through with force if success is to be achieved." Will you remain in the tomb because it's comfortable, because it's what you know? Or will you step through the opening given to you into the unknown, into the realm of possibility with God? The body of Christ must push past mental hindrances with force and choose to believe in faith if she is ever to become who she was always created to be in Christ.

Many of us have been hidden in caves for a time, a season of maturing. Will we allow that cave to actually become our tomb and hold us in death? Or will we step out into the light no matter how painful it is to push past our limited mindsets and decide to believe for the impossible and to live. Many are wrestling with depression, insomnia, and complacency. Sometimes if we are honest, it's easier to complain about our pasts and current situations than it is to choose to have faith and hope for our futures. We can inadvertently create a death hold on ourselves by our closed minds and religious and worldly thinking. But if we can just allow the King of kings and Lord of lords to work in us and reveal *his* hope for our futures, *his* faith in our fulfilled destinies, we can be free from those death holds and embrace this resurrection life that awaits us. We need only to take hold of it, welcome the resurrection in our lives. I believe most of us understand what it means to die to the self, yet we lack understanding in what it truly means to live this resurrection realm. The key is the resurrection already exists in you as a believer. It's already a part of you the moment you received Jesus as your Savior.

It only needs to be unlocked within you. It is unlocked in faith and trust in God.

> Then David got up from the ground. After he had washed, put on lotions and changed his clothes, he went into the house of the LORD and worshiped. Then he went to his own house, and at his request they served him food, and he ate. His servants asked him, "Why are you acting this way? While the child was alive, you fasted and wept, but now that the child is dead, you get up and eat!" He answered, "While the child was still alive, I fasted and wept. I thought, 'Who knows? The LORD may be gracious to me and let the child live.' But now that he is dead, why should I fast? Can I bring him back again? I will go to him, but he will not return to me."
>
> 2 Samuel 12:20–23

King David wept over his consequences in hopes that God might change his mind. But when the will of God played out, he decided to take off the sackcloth and clean himself up, and he began to eat again, to fill himself up again. The servants were surprised that he did not weep over the end result. David's response was that he wept while there was time to change a situation, but when God's will was accomplished, he chose to receive God's will, not his own. He aligned himself with God's decision and chose not to stay in the past and continue to mourn for something that was gone. God had rendered his decision. And David chose to believe that God knew best. He decided to move forward and to weep no more. He made a conscious choice to continue to live again no matter what his feelings told him or his circumstances dictated. By choosing to live, a new life was created between him and his wife, and God blessed them with another child. Was it wrong for David to weep, to mourn? No, not at all. For Scripture reveals there is "a time to weep and a time to laugh, a time to mourn and a time to dance" (Ecclesiastes 3:4). It's when we continue holding onto the past season when the new season has been released upon us that it becomes an issue for us. When we hang onto past grievances, past failures, past broken promises, past unfulfilled dreams, and past disappointments, we remain in the dark tomb secluded from everyone and everything, and we sit and waste away in a spiritual death.

I have heard so many times through ministers about the death and resurrection of Jesus and many thoughts and opinions on it. Some feel it is the death that holds the key; many feel it's the suffering and judgment the Lord took upon himself for us. But others say, and I agree with this statement, that it's not just all about the death, the suffering, or the resurrection. It's the combination that makes it so miraculous and so powerful. The death of Jesus would mean nothing without the resurrection. It does us no good to continually die to our flesh patterns and lay ourselves down if we do not decide to live in the truth, the light, the life of Jesus Christ. When something is emptied or removed, it is to make room for something new. We can release things all day long, but it's for the purpose of being able to embrace and make room for the new. We decrease in ourselves that we may increase in him. God exchanges what we offer for what he has to offer. As long as we remain in the tomb, we will never fill ourselves up with the life God has for us, what he sacrificed to give to us. God never takes away unless he has something to exchange it with. When we give, we open ourselves to receive. It's a spiritual law. God says, "Come to me, all you who are weary and burdened, and I will give you rest. Take my yoke upon you and learn from me, for I am gentle and humble in heart, and you will find rest for your souls. For my yoke is easy and my burden is light"(Matthew 11:28–30). It's another exchange. He exchanged your burdens for his and your death walk for his resurrected life walk. In exchange for dying to your flesh, you received Jesus' life in you. When you died to the old man (sinful nature), you became a new creation.

The devil wants to continually remind you that you are not a new creation and that you didn't receive Christ's inheritance, including his resurrection. He wants to convince your mind that you are still locked in a tomb. Well, as we know from God's Word, the devil is a liar and a deceiver. "He was a murderer from the beginning, not holding to the truth, for there is no truth in him. When he lies, he speaks his native language, for he is a liar and the father of lies" (John 8:44). It's all he knows how to do, which is to convince you that God's Word is not true by altering circumstances and feelings and situations to show you the exact opposite of what God has told you. And he is really good. Satan is a pro at what he does. His other favorite thing to do is to get you to deceive yourself and keep you in a death grip. "Let him not deceive himself by trusting what is worthless, for he will get nothing in return" (Job15:31). This is where your faith needs to be elevated to new heights, when the circumstances show you the opposite of what God has promised and when your mind tells you the opposite of what God's Word says and his character reveals. This is an opportunity for you to take God's Word and stand on it, to believe him for the impossible. God wants to take your faith to new levels all the time. It is for the purpose that you would operate in God's faith level!

> Now Thomas (called Didymus), one of the Twelve, was not with the disciples when Jesus came. So the other disciples told him, "We have seen the Lord!" But he said to them, "Unless I see the nail marks in his hands and put my finger where the nails were, and put my hand into his side, I will not believe it." A week later his disciples were in the house again, and Thomas was with them. Though the doors were locked, Jesus came and stood among them and said, "Peace be with you!" Then he said to Thomas, "Put your finger here; see my hands. Reach out your hand and put it into my side. Stop doubting and believe." Thomas said to him, "My Lord and my God!"
>
> John 20: 24–28

When we look at the disciple Thomas, we see an example of one who needed to see that this man standing before him was actually his friend and mentor Jesus. Thomas couldn't believe until Jesus told him to touch his nail-scarred hands and place his hand in his wounded side. Suddenly the resurrection became a reality for even Thomas, someone who was hard to convince. Even better, Thomas now not only saw Jesus as his friend and mentor, but he saw him as his Savior! Any mind limitations he had of Jesus were completely obliterated at that moment. Even those that are hard to convince will see the resurrection of God upon your life. They get to be witnesses to the power of God in and upon your life, and God will use this to bring many unbelieving into the kingdom. They too will suddenly become convinced that this Jesus you serve is the Messiah, the Savior. But blessed are you who believe without having to see with your natural eyes (John 20:29)! You can wait for God to show your natural eyes before you step out of your tomb, or you can choose to believe in your calling, in his word, in your inheritance, in your position in Christ. You can choose to believe that this is your moment to step out in faith and allow God to meet you. Once the stone has been removed, how long you remain in the tomb is completely up to you.

Jesus not only chose to walk from the tomb, but by faith he went and appeared to those who had witnessed his death and his decrease and showed them he was in fact alive and well. No longer held captive by death he was now a conqueror over death's hold on him. I believe each person Jesus came to show himself to received that resurrection by faith at that very moment. Others who doubt around you will see and know that God has resurrected you. You get to be a testimony unto the resurrection power of Christ. By faith will you take hold of that realm of truly living?

Lot's wife could not resist looking at her past and what she had lost. God gave the command through his angels to not look back. What God had to offer Lot and his family was far greater than what they had. They needed to trust that *he* was their new land, their future. But Lot's wife could not let go, and she looked back at the destruction of her city of Sodom and its sister city, Gomorrah, and she was turned into a pillar of salt (Genesis 19:1–26). Lot's wife never left her "tomb." And in doing so, she forfeited her future, her resurrection with God.

God is removing things from the past such as old patterns, habits, relationships, and connections, and he is repositioning you to receive the *new*. The old clothing, the old attitudes, the old limitations cannot enter into your resurrection with you. It's okay to grieve it for a moment, but do not stay there and become one with the tomb. It was never created to house you, only to rest in for a time, a season. You were not created to die but to live! God wants every part of our hearts, our minds and our spirits to grasp this resurrection life. To resurrect means to breathe new life into, to restart, to revitalize, to resuscitate, and restore to life.

Will you make a decision today to believe that God has a resurrection life available *in* you? In faith will you walk out of the tomb, trust and embrace whatever God has in store for you no matter what it looks or feels like? Or will you stay in the comfort of your tomb and never enter into your inheritance that was set aside just for you? Seize your moment, saints. The stone has been rolled away. By faith it's up to you to release the resurrection that has always been a part of you lying in wait for your *kairos* moment— God's appointed time!

Epilogue

My prayer is that after reading these Holy Spirit–inspired writings you will discover greater revelation of your heavenly Father and his love, grace, and mercy for you. I hope as a believer that this book has reignited your passion to go forth in the name of the Lord assured of your victory in Christ Jesus to fulfill the destiny to which he has called you.

If you are reading this as someone who has never met Jesus Christ, I thank you for taking the time to read this book and hope that it has illuminated your heart, mind, and spirit to the truth, life, power and love of Jesus Christ. If you would like to know him more, then please pray the following prayer:

> Jesus,
>
> Your Word says that anyone who calls on your name shall be saved. I call to you today and ask forgiveness of those things of which I know of and those things of which I am unaware I have sinned. Be my Lord and my Savior. I receive the life you gave for me on the cross and I desire to walk in the

fullness of your resurrection for me. I now believe that I am no longer dead but that I have everlasting life with you because I am no longer called a sinner but a son/daughter of the kingdom of heaven.

In Jesus' name, Amen.

Welcome to the beginning of your life, my newly beloved brother/sister in the faith! I rejoice with you and all the angels in heaven for your entrance into an everlasting abundant life. Enjoy discovering who you are in Christ and all that he wants to accomplish in you and through you. Blessings!

Bibliography

All scriptures referenced are in New International Version (NIV) and New Living Translation (NLT)

Books

The Prophet's Dictionary: The Ultimate Guide to Supernatural Wisdom by Paula A. Price, Ph.D, revised edition 2006

Internet

Bible Gateway.com, 1995–2008, http://www.Biblegateway.com

Bible.com, Inc., 1995–2005, http://www.Bible.com

Wikipedia, the Free Encyclopedia, English version, Wikimedia Foundation, http://en.wikipedia.org

Author Jeanette C Morgan resides in Northern California
and can be contacted regarding *The Voice That Must Be
Heard* at: jeanettecmorgan@yahoo.com